MARXISM IN THE
TWENTIETH
CENTURY

Roger Garaudy

MARXISM IN THE TWENTIETH CENTURY

Translated by René Hague

COLLINS

ST JAMES'S PLACE, LONDON
1970

S.B.N. 00 215512 5

© Editions La Palatine, Paris-Genève, 1970
© in the English translation 1969
William Collins Sons & Co. Ltd., London
and Charles Scribner's Sons, New York

Printed in Great Britain by
Collins Clear-Type Press
London and Glasgow

'Por eso no me espero de regreso
No soy de los que vuelven de la luz.'

Pablo Neruda. *'Sonata Critica'*,
Memorial de Isla Negra

Contents

Introduction

It is sometimes much more difficult to state a problem correctly than it is to find a solution for it.

In this last third of the twentieth century the pace of development in human relationships, in man's knowledge and power, is such as to produce a profound change in the ancient 'data' of our problems.

In Apocalyptic times there can be no set rules to govern our thought.

We must therefore, as Pastor Dietrich Bonhoeffer wrote in 1944, 'take the risk of saying things that are open to dispute, provided that vital problems are thereby raised.'

This fundamental consideration is particularly essential for Marxists precisely because Marxism is not one of a number of philosophies but an awareness of the underlying movement that governs our history, the Promethean enterprise of taking control of the process of development and of deliberately building up the future. The fact that Marxism is the *sense* of our century imposes a personal responsibility on every Marxist.

Marxism has given proof of its fruitfulness and creative effectiveness in countless practical fields. It has transformed the economic and social life of vast countries; it has allowed millions of men, enslaved for thousands of years, to have access to culture and to win for themselves living conditions that are at last human. How then is it that, in this tempestuous world of the twentieth century, Marxist philosophy, like the sleeping beauty, has been wrapped in slumber for the last twenty-five years?

It got off to a flying start. Marx and Engels made man

9

sharply aware of his creative potentialities and gave the working class a programme for building up a society that would allow man to attain the fullness of his development; and with it, they gave a technique which is both a fighting technique and a scientific technique for establishing this society.

This teaching had begun to organise the class war of the proletariat throughout the world, and to inspire complete confidence in the victory of the labour movement; but as early as 1890, during the period of a relatively peaceful development of the capitalist world, this current, with the new impetus it gave to thought and action, first began to stagnate in an opportunist dogmatism that was contaminated by the prevailing positivism and scientism.

Lenin restored to Marxism its revolutionary vitality both by a return to fundamentals which brought out the essence of Marxism, a concept of the world which provides the basis for a methodology of historical initiative, and by a scientific analysis of the real nature of his time: scientific, precisely because it did not try to interpret events as though they were no more than the fulfilment of a scenario written fifty years earlier, but rather to comprehend what was new in them.

In his opposition to all forms of dogmatism, which lead to a fatalistic view of history, to 'economism' and 'spontaneity', Lenin redisclosed the fundamental inspiration and the living soul of Marxist thought. 'The essential point in Marx's doctrine is that it has brought out the universal role in history of the proletariat as the creator of socialist society,' wrote Lenin at the beginning of his study of 'the historic destinies of the teaching of Karl Marx.'

Against all interpretations of Marxism that, under the pretext of objectivity, confuse 'scientific' history with a history in which the future is already laid down and from which man is absent, Lenin put forward the authentically Marxist concept of historical initiative.

In a preface written in February 1907 for the Russian edition of Marx's letters to Kugelmann, Lenin first refers to Marx's illusions about the 1848 revolution, and then castigates 'the pedants of Marxism who think that all this is a load of moralistic nonsense, romanticism, lack of realism. No, gentlemen,' answers Lenin, 'it is the union of revolutionary theory with revolutionary politics' without which one falls, in company with the Plekhanovs and the Kautskys, into a concept of 'objectivity' which is a theoretical justification of opportunism. 'That theory is not Marxist which passes from observation of an objective situation to justification of the existing state of affairs.'

Lenin contrasts Plekhanov's position when, after the Russian revolution in December 1905, he said that they should not have taken up arms, with Marx's attitude to the Commune in Paris.

In September 1870, more than six months before the Commune, Marx, in his address to the International, warned the French workers against the nationalist illusions that threatened to start 1792 over again, and showed that the rising had no hope of success. But when it actually began in March 1871, he did not try (Lenin tells us) 'to lecture his Proudhonian or Blanquist opponents who were at the head of the Commune.' He did not grumble, 'I told you so, you should not have taken up arms.' 'No, on 12th April 1871 he wrote an enthusiastic letter to Kugelmann, a letter which one would like to see pinned up on the wall of every Russian Communist, of every worker who can read . . . He is full of praise for these heroic Parisian workers following the lead of the Proudhonians and Blanquists. "What *historical initiative* and what a capacity for sacrifice they showed." ' And Lenin goes on to say that what Marx values above all is the *historical initiative* of the masses. 'Ah, how they would laugh at Marx, our present-day "pundits" of Marxism, our "realists", who denounce revolutionary romanticism in the Russia of 1906-7. How, in the name of materialism, of economism, of the struggle against utopia, they would ridicule the man who so admired this attempt to storm the heavens.'

Marx himself made a close study of the technique of revolution. Instead of repeating, like the dogmatic Plekhanov, that there should have been no armed rising, he urged offensive action. 'There should have been an immediate march on Versailles.' And a few days later he said that the Central Committee of the Commune surrendered its plenary powers too soon.

When Kugelmann expressed his doubts to Marx, spoke of a hopeless enterprise, and opposed realism to romanticism, Marx immediately answered (on 17th April 1871), 'World history would indeed be very easy to make if the struggle were taken up only on condition of infallibly favourable chances' (*Selected Works*, p. 681).

This sharp awareness of what is fundamental in Marxism and of what is new in history enabled Lenin to undertake and carry through the October revolution, which was not only the beginning of hope for the oppressed of the whole world but also, for all those whose hearts and minds are set on the future, the greatest spiritual event at the dawn of the twentieth century.

The Leninist enterprise bore such rich cultural fruit that it was distinguished by an outburst of dazzling works. The twenties witnessed the appearance of the poems of Alexander Blok and Maiakovski, the paintings of Kandinsky and Malevitch, the novels of Gorki and Alexis Tolstoi, and the films of Eisenstein.

People who came to manhood in the period between the two world wars and were awake to what was then being born, lived in an exhilarating atmosphere: the Bolsheviks' struggle against the attack of fourteen nations ended in victory; in the course of a few years the epic of the five-year plans transformed an economically and technically backward country into one of the leading world powers. Later, facing the flood of the Nazi onslaught, this heroic people

alone stood free while nearly the whole of Europe was enslaved, and at Stalingrad saved the world from reverting for
a thousand years to barbarism. And then again there came
the rebuilding of thousands of towns that had been destroyed,
and man's first achievements in space as he burst out into the
cosmos.

That story contains the solid foundation on which to base,
the enduring landmarks within which to contain, our critical
judgment.

To this must be added all the hopes born of this new life:
the Spanish war which made of that people the first of the
patriotic resistances against Hitlerian fascism, and the outstanding part played in the struggle for freedom against
Nazism by the Communist parties: the Long March and the
triumph, in the middle of the century, of the Chinese revolution, and, at the other end of the world, Cuba, whose
revolutionary romanticism linked hands with Marxism-
Leninism.

Faced with what was in process of birth and development,
the world was entering an agonising era: the 1914-18 war
had already challenged many values; the Versailles treaties
were creating new hotbeds of war; the horror of colonialism
was reaching—in the inter-war period—its culminating point;
the 1929 crisis swept away the last illusions about an economic order that allowed the law of the jungle to prevail in
a world of iron.

This total crisis was ultimately overcome only by a 'total
war', a concept that was first hammered out by Ludendorff,
and of which Hitlerism was the most complete, though by no
means the only, expression. The final abandonment of any
distinction between civil and military was inaugurated at
Guernica and asserted at Hiroshima.

The capitalist system, in its most typical, richest and most
powerful expression, that of the U.S.A., failed to prove that
it could ensure prosperity, even for a single nation, without
a policy of armament and war, without the exploitation of

whole continents such as that of Latin America. It failed to prove that it was capable of realising a democracy, from the MacCarthy-ist inquisition to the racialist pogroms of Los Angeles, from Guatemala to Vietnam.

We were fighting absolute evil: how, then, could we not feel that our cause was the cause of absolute good? So we came to accept this Manichean view of the world; on the one side, the whole of evil and, in virtue of a world-embracing concept of decadence, the denial of any possibility of seeing the birth of the least human value, even artistic, from a world that was in fact going rotten; on the other side, the whole of good, without shades or half-tones, and, in the name of party spirit, the rejection of any critical perspective. So much so, indeed, that without its even being imposed on us, we enthusiastically welcomed Stalinist dogmatism.

The entire system was synthesised in twenty dazzling pages which were held to contain the whole of philosophical wisdom. After 'Latin without tears' we had 'instant Greek'; we had philosophy brought within every man's reach in three easy lessons. Ontology: the three principles of materialism. Logic: the four laws of dialectics. Philosophy of history: the five stages of the class war.

So long as this concept prevails, there is no Marxist philosophy; all there is, is a sort of scholasticism which claims to answer all questions without knowing the nature of any of them, running from biology to aesthetics by way of agriculture and chemistry. Such success as was achieved, was not due to, but rather in spite of, this theology. In physics the 'philosophers' were silenced so that the scientists could get on with their work in disciplines whose practical demands, most fortunately, were sufficiently insistent to overrule the anathemas of this scholasticism—as, for example, in the case of cybernetics, which was initially classed as a 'bourgeois science'. Far from being a guide to research, this concept of dialectics and of philosophy in general acted as a brake upon it.

Nevertheless, the building up of socialism was carried on in accordance with the general plan laid down by Lenin, and political life was only partially deranged by this mistaken theorising; a first reason for this was that the practical demands of the class war and the national traditions of the proletariat in European countries led to heroic and clear-cut struggles, and these called for a breaking down, in fact, of the dogmatic scheme which affected its essential points.

Lenin, for example, had taught that the very activities of the militants would have no meaning nor basis if the coming of socialism was already guaranteed by some external necessity. As against the theories of 'economism' and 'spontaneity', he emphasised the importance of the 'subjective element', that is of consciousness, in revolutionary action.

The fight in the French Communist party against fatalistic dogmatism was a permanent feature in the work of Maurice Thorez, who in 1934 wrote, 'There is nothing inevitable in the crushing of capitalism' (*Oeuvres*, Vol. VI, p. 12). Again in 1950, 'War is not inevitable'; 'Destitution is not inevitable', he wrote in 1956, in his studies on pauperisation, in which he contests 'the concept of an iron law, of an inevitability that is a dead weight on the working class' (*Cahiers du Communisme*, 1957, No. 5, p. 685). It was this that made possible the great historical initiatives of his life, such as the Popular Front, and the 'outstretched hand' offered to Christians, the *Front français*, whose soundness was to be vindicated in the Resistance, the liberation and the renascence of France.

It nevertheless remains true that, while the movement was able, in essentials, to pursue its course, it was at the cost of a terrible human wastage: it meant the eclipse, for a quarter of a century, of the fundamental, critical and practical, that is to say scientific, inspiration of Marxism, in favour of a concept of the world and of knowledge that had become dogmatic and theological—and for this a heavy price had to be paid in millions of human lives.

Inquisition is the daughter of dogmatism.

As soon as one abandons the indivisibly scientific and humanist attitude and accepts the myth of an absolute truth, transcending the men who live it and create it in the day-to-day activities that make up their history, murderous and authoritarian methods are the inevitable fruit of the necessity to impose that truth from above.

Violations of democracy in the party and the state necessarily stem from this theological concept of the world, of historical development and of human thought.

For a long time a combination of historical circumstances delayed the realisation of this cardinal error. The Soviet Union was an entrenched camp. The régimes of the jungle, with their thirst for plunder, which were responsible for the wholesale slaughter of the first world war, and for the colonialist annihilation of the peoples and civilisation of three continents, were waging a military, economic and ideological war to the death against the U.S.S.R.

We had no choice. Unless we passionately defended the hope springing from the October revolution, we were inevitably playing into the hands of all the forces that were destroying man. Millions of men gladly and manfully offered up life or liberty in this battle, and not one of them can regret his sacrifice. 'If it had to be done again,' said Péri, 'I'd retrace the same road.' And every one of us, I believe, can say the same. Those of us who survived the maquis, the prisons or the concentration camps, would be ready, even with a perfectly clear awareness of the conditions in which socialism was established, to take up the same attitude in the face of the same enemy; and we would reject with equal vigour his condemning in socialism a violence that contradicts the principles of socialism, whereas that violence is the internal law of development of the capitalism which fights it.

As for those who give their anti-communism a spiritual motivation, they would do well to consider the real meaning of a one-track spirituality which is silent when confronted with Batista's massacres and yet raises a cry of persecution under Fidel Castro, which tries to rouse the passions of Christians by telling them about the 'silenced churches', and yet has nothing to say about, or even gives its blessing to, the terror and the tortures of the highly 'Christian' régimes of Salazar or Franco.

We were aware of all this, and we had to face it. In the end the implacable logic of battle identified the necessity for international solidarity with unconditional acceptance, en bloc, of what issued from our camp. We came to distinguish no longer between the violence necessary to counter the enemy's violence and violence blindly exerted against our own men and our own ideas. The same inexorable logic led us to reduce the necessary class and party spirit to a single one of its components: the spirit of discipline, which becomes an abstraction as soon as it is divorced from the spirit of initiative and of criticism. Science became a matter of discipline, instead of discipline being a matter of science.

And what about the position today?

The twentieth Congress of the Communist Party of the U.S.S.R. marked the beginning of a tragic but vitalising awakening.

By drawing up a balance sheet of what had been gained and won, and of the prospects opening up for the future, but also by showing in what conditions this had been effected, it made possible a new departure.

Whatever the mistakes later made by Nikita Kruschev, and in spite of his tendency to repeat mistakes whose origin and disastrous consequences he had nevertheless made clear, he had this unprecedented merit: that at last he fundamentally challenged, in the eyes of the whole world, a concept and methods that had led a socialist régime to rob itself of the unique treasure represented by the personal historic initiative of millions of citizens and fighters, to shed their blood in violation of the rules of democracy in party and state, and even to use dogmatised theory as an ideology to justify this crime against socialism.

Confronted by these revelations, and not for a moment forgetting the prospects for the future they at the same time opened up, it happened that I re-read, as though it were a message addressed to me personally, Hegel's sombre passage in his *Phenomenology of Mind* (tr. J. B. Baillie, 1931, p. 237): 'This consciousness was not in peril and fear for this element or that, nor for this or that moment of time, it was afraid for its entire being; it felt the fear of death, the sovereign master. It has been in that experience melted to its inmost soul, has trembled throughout its every fibre, and all that was fixed and steadfast has quaked within it.'

For a soul, the fear of death is the fear of losing its motives for living and acting: and there is no reason why one should not admit that for a moment, on the morrow of the twentieth Congress, one understood just what this utter vital bewilderment could be. This was something one had never experienced in prison or concentration camps.

It was when we had passed this 'nightmare turning point' that we set out to reconquer our certain beliefs; not in a mood of scepticism or disillusionment, not with our minds made up to believe no longer, but determined to believe no longer except with our eyes open. As Pushkin wrote, 'The blows of the hammer shatter glass and forge iron.'

This test of the twentieth Congress, far from destroying our hopes and certainties, had the opposite effect of making possible a third flowering for Marxist philosophy.

It is not, however, by turning over the page too quickly and so neglecting to expose all the roots of evil, nor by thus failing correctly to apportion responsibility or to demand a profound analysis of the causes that produced the former blindness, that this fresh start can be made possible.

For my own part, I have for the last ten years been experiencing this gnawing need exactly to assess my responsibilities, both theoretical and practical. Throughout this book, accordingly, I am speaking not in the name of the Political Bureau of the French Communist Party, but in my own individual name: it is only my own self that I am committing, even though I am writing with an acute sense of my duty, as a philosopher, to my Party and its Political Bureau, of which I have the responsibility and honour of being a member.

For to accept uncritically Stalin's concepts in philosophy (as I did, for example, in my thesis on the materialist theory of knowledge), with all the consequences it entails for the sciences from genetics to chemistry, for the arts from music to painting, was more than an error in theory: approval of condemnations issued in the name of official dogmas facilitated, by giving them an international warrant, the task of those who prevented some particular person from writing, painting, or even living.

If we are to make it impossible for this to happen again, we must make a collective, and hence a public, effort fully and frankly to expose the roots of error, and to rediscover, at a new stage in history, the fundamental inspiration of Marxism.

It is the aim of this book to make a contribution, on the theoretical plane, to this effort.

CHAPTER ONE

The Terms of the Problems in this Last Third of the Twentieth Century

*

Cultural problems present themselves today in new historical conditions that call for a great creative effort.

During these last two decades the rhythm of history has accelerated in a way that has no precedent.

Three massive facts dominate this situation:

1. The staggering developments of the sciences and technology.

2. The building-up of socialism on the road to becoming a world-wide system.

3. The decolonisation of two continents, Asia and Africa.

It is no longer a question of a quantitative change: of a number of further discoveries, of some further advances in socialism, of some colonies achieving independence. Since the second world war there has been a qualitative change.

This means that we are faced by problems that have never arisen before, and we have to appreciate the scale of the effort that must be made if we are to bring Marxism up to the measure of such requirements.

Our awareness lags behind history. If we wish to find a way of catching up on this delay we must be fully conscious of it; only so will Marxism be able successfully to construct the new synthesis, the demand for which is expressed in all the great currents of thought today. Everyone feels that there is a gap between historical reality and our awareness of it. The need for an '*aggiornamento*', for bringing things up to date, is not confined to Catholics alone; it is a general phenomenon.

Starting from the three great facts enumerated above, how do the problems present themselves?

*

Man's power over nature has increased more in twenty years than it did during the last twenty centuries.

A number of scientific and technical discoveries are the basis of this revolution.

The most spectacular fact is the manufacture of the atomic and thermonuclear bomb. At Hiroshima in 1945 it amounted to no more than a means of destruction more violent than others, but ten years later a qualitative change was effected. With the stocks of bombs now in existence, it has become technically possible, if they are methodically distributed, to wipe out every trace of life on earth. The epic story of man, which began a million years ago, could well draw to a close.

The second consequence of these discoveries is equally important: human history has opened up for itself prospects to which there are no limits. Only thirty years ago it was possible to foresee the time when our planet's stocks of energy —coal, oil—would be exhausted. Now, with the extension of the disintegration of matter, it will no longer be possible to assign any limits to man's power and wealth.

A third consequence of these discoveries concerns the global destiny of mankind. The cooling of the sun and the earth used to make it possible to envisage a term to the life of the human species on a globe that would become un-inhabitable. The first steps in cosmonautics and the energy-potentials of the disintegration of matter now allow us to dismiss that prospect. In virtue of its conquests, our species can dream of a real immortality.

A new science, born from the synthesis of the study of the phenomena of autoregulation and the calculus of probabilities was inaugurated about 1949 with the publication of Norbert Wiener's book on cybernetics; and in hardly a decade this has found far-reaching applications.

What we have witnessed is not a mere quantitative change, no more than one further stage in mechanical development. Hitherto, from the discoveries of fire and the chipping of stone to those of steam, the internal combustion engine and electricity, the object of the tool and later of the machine, whatever improvements they underwent, was to increase man's *physical* strength, to take the place of manual work, to make it quicker and more efficient.

From now on, the change is qualitative: it is a question of finding a substitute for certain forms of man's mental work.

For example, in order to control the course of a satellite, it is necessary to calculate its trajectory at every moment. These operations would require dozens of highly qualified mathematicians working for months on end: and when they had finished, the satellite would be miles away and their work would be useless.

Electronic computers can carry out, with complete accuracy, millions of complex operations a second, and the unit of time has become the 'nano-second' (10^{-9} second, one thousand millionth of a second).

The electronic computer is not the super-market's cash register with simply an improved calculating machine. No: it screens the solutions and even informs the scientist if he has expressed the problem incorrectly at the start.

Its application is being extended in every field.

In the U.S.A. the electronic device 'Geda' automatically controls the production and distribution of electric power from nine generating stations . . . It monitors the quantity of electricity used; it works out the cost of coal per factory, the heat-value of the coal and its relative degree of humidity, the characteristics of the electric mains, etc.

In January 1964 an electronic computer was used in Moscow to determine the best technical variation for the erection of a building. In March 1964 a device was under construction in the naval ship-yard at Leningrad which would automatically lead ships to the fishing grounds and control the operations of catching and processing the fish.

A qualitative change has similarly been effected in communications and telecommunications.

For close on 2,000 years there was little change. It took Julius Cæsar and Napoleon almost the same time to travel from Paris to Rome. Their rate of progress was determined by the speed of a horse and the organisation of relays. Steam and the railways brought no more than a quantitative change; the journey was made three or four times as quickly.

Aviation effects another quantitative change, with a seven or eightfold increase in speed. With the space rocket, however, we move into a new scale, that of the movement of the stars. The speed of a satellite is far greater than that of the earth's rotation. At one step we have a multiplication not by three or four, by seven or by nine, but by a hundred or a thousand.

Aviation has made man capable of a planetary life. He is now beginning a new career, that of a cosmic destiny.

For a long time the communication of information kept pace with human communication. The mail travelled at the speed of the horse. Today, not only is there the technical possibility of an instantaneous presentation of news over the whole world, but it has become a mass phenomenon through the extremely rapid increase in the last ten years in the number of radio and television receivers: Eurovision, worldvision via Telstar, and, already, photographs taken on the moon.

This system of disseminating information has produced a profound revolution in the conditions governing political propaganda, as it has in education and culture.

In *biology* there have been more new discoveries in ten years than in the whole period from Hippocrates to Claude Bernard.

Discoveries that entail a qualitative change have been made since 1954.

At the beginning of this century Loeb thought that science's long-term targets were:

the synthesis of life;

control of the evolution of species.

Now, with the synthesis of nucleotids capable of reproducing themselves, begun in 1954 by Ochoa and Kornberg, and the controlled modifications of these chains of nucleotids effected by Watson and Crick, these targets are in process of being achieved.

Many indications justify us in thinking that discoveries in biology are going to be made in the last third of this century which will be no less important than those made in physics during the first two thirds.

Man is now becoming not simply 'evolution conscious of itself' but evolution master of itself; he is becoming one of the agents of evolution. He is becoming capable of modifying heredity and biologically steering man's potentialities. This is raising a problem within science itself, a moral problem, a problem of ends; on the ground of what values shall we choose the aptitudes to be developed?

These are but a few examples of the changes that have been introduced.

They raise in an acute form the problem of education, of assimilation, of the diffusion and control of what has been gained.

To emphasise no more than the breadth of the questions raised, we should recall three facts:

at the present moment there are as many creative scientists living as the total number that have existed since the beginnings of mankind (Auger Report to the scientific research section of Unesco);

the quantity of human knowledge has doubled in the last eight years (in the volume of scientific publications, works of research, learned periodicals, leaving out of account popular presentations);

the time-lag between a basic discovery and its mass practical application is being fantastically cut down: in the case of photography it was 112 years, of the telephone 56, of transistors 5.

These facts bring out the breadth of the problems.

A philosophical problem. Engels said that materialism must change its form with every great discovery that marks a new epoch in the history of the sciences. Lenin made a gigantic effort to think in terms of the science of his day. Consider, then, what an infinitely greater effort we shall have to make today if we are to bring Marxist philosophy up to the present level of scientific development.

A political problem. This staggering increase in our technical mastery of nature entrusts to a few handfuls of men a fund of knowledge and an organisation that gives them a terrifying power. This technocratic cleavage between the managers and the masses is the law in monopolistic régimes in which the concentration of resources is a class matter. In fundamentally different conditions, the objective difficulties created by this situation raise problems for the development of a true socialist democracy.

An educational problem. If the sum total of knowledge has doubled in eight or ten years, the addition of one chapter to the curriculum of school-leaving forms is not enough to give young people even a summary knowledge of what is being created. There must be a fundamental re-thinking of the curricula, and the problem of extra-scholastic culture takes on a new urgency.

*

The establishment of socialism created the conditions for an unprecedented flowering of culture and the arts.

In the first place, because with the struggle of the working class, guided and directed by a Marxist-Leninist party, the divorce between work and culture began to be overcome.

Secondly, because the victory of the working class and the dictatorship of the proletariat make it possible to put an end to a régime which turns cultural values into commodity values.

Finally, because socialist democracy offers every man, and every child, the means fully to develop the human riches he contains within himself, and thereby the possibility of attaining an understanding of, and the power to create, works of culture.

If culture begins with work and develops with it, then every great change in the organisation of social labour and production-relationships entails a profound change in culture and the conditions of its development.

One of the principal characteristics of socialism is that, unlike capitalism, because of its class nature, because of the abolition of private ownership of the means of production, it becomes possible, for the first time in human history, to have *a real planning of social labour*.

When plans are no longer both directed by profit and hampered by it, when they are no longer inspired by the interests of a few individuals (the owners of the means of production), but by the real needs of all men, a great cultural and moral change begins to be produced in mankind: for the first time man can be conscious of the aims that are being pursued. Man can take over evolution, whose driving force is no longer *nature*, the brutish confrontation of conflicting interests, but *culture*, the knowledge of the ends and means of human development.

Communism makes it possible to go beyond the limited projects of the succession of exploiting classes, and to conceive a universal project: with communism, that is to say when *production relationships and state relationships* have been overcome, it will be possible for properly human relationships to come into being. Everyone will be able to live the life of all the others and, for the first time, one human world will form a 'totality'.

Such is the theoretical line of development—the 'dotted line' drawn by Marx and Engels.

The real historical development of the Soviet Union and of the countries that are building up socialism has had a decisive effect on the future of culture all over the world. The confidence of millions of men in the possibility of re-building human relationships, of conceiving human relationships other than those of capitalism and other class societies—in a word, the possibility of socialism—has become a widely accepted certainty, even if, for many people, the idea of socialism is still vague and blurred.

However, the real historical development of socialism has proved to be more fruitful than its theoretical trajectory.

In particular, in what relates to the organisation of social labour, planning problems are infinitely more complex today than they were forty or even twenty years ago.

In the Soviet Union, for example, the problem in planning was initially the creation of the technical and economic foundations of socialism.

At first, a backwardness in comparison with capitalist countries had to be overcome: from the point of view both of the end and of the methods and means, the plan was in a way moulded or taken as a blueprint from the development of the big industrialised countries.

The end was the creation of means of defence and possibilities of consumption.

The means, the giving of an absolute priority to heavy industry; to the production of the means of production in order to meet the demands of defence and future consumption.

These demands entailed an ethic, an aesthetic, and a pedagogy. Everything that contributes to the achievement of this great end is right and proper.

In the first place, a high-minded morality, based on self-denial, discipline, sacrifice, the gift of self, which found expression on all the fronts in the civil war and the fight against intervention, and later in the work put into the great construction yards of the five-year plans, and then again in the war against Hitlerian fascism.

In aesthetics, the greatest works of the period were those which extolled the same end and contributed to it: from *Chapaiev* to Gladkov's *Cement*, from Alexis Tolstoi's *Road to Calvary* to Fadeiev's *Young Guard*, from Makarenko's *Road to Life* to Sholokov's *The Virgin Soil Upturned*.

The pedagogy corresponding to this period was that which at the same time was founded on this ethic of discipline and sacrifice, and was centred on the rapid assimilation of natural sciences and technical skills.

It is in no way paradoxical that it was after the twentieth Congress, that is to say after it was possible to draw up an impressive balance sheet of the victories won, that difficulties made themselves felt in the socialist world.

It would be a mistake to believe that it was the denunciation of Stalin that raised the difficulties, it was, on the contrary, the importance of the victories that had been won.

The raising of the standard of living in the countries that were building up socialism, the rapid extension of education, the very progress of socialisation in institutions and man-ners—in one word, it was the success of socialism which had created new demands.

The central theoretical problem, starting from which the problems of social organisation of work and planning are re-thought, *is the problem of the role of commodity relationships and of the operation of the law of value in the socialist economy.*

The method for making proper allowance for this consists in starting from the very principle of the socialist régime and from the totality of the conditions in which it is realised.

The starting point is the fact that socialism is a transition régime between capitalism and communism.

In the capitalist régime commodity relationships control practically all human relationships, and the blind working of the law of value is the driving force behind development.

In a communist régime commodity relationships between

men have disappeared, and the law of value is no more than an instrument of national accountancy.

In a socialist régime there is a *contradiction* between these two extreme terms: between the project of a direct and centralised planning at the end of which all human relationships will become free and open, and commodity relationships which are still objectively subject to the law of value.

Starting from this over-all analysis of the nature of socialism, Professor Sik, of Prague, has shown that the reason for the existence of commodity relationships in a socialist régime is precisely this *contradiction* between the fundamental social co-operation made possible by the coming of socialism, and the character of work and consumption: this gives rise to interests and incentives shared by individuals and groups that are not yet identified with the general interest of society as a whole.

In this period commodity relationships and the operation of the law of value make it possible to reconcile the interests of groups asserting themselves within the framework of a planned social co-operation.

Following this course, two systematic errors were possible:

on the one hand the sectarian error which consists in expecting every citizen in the socialist society to behave as though he were already a citizen in the communist society, for whom conscience and the moral incentive are determining forces, and in considering the material incentive as a mere survival from the old capitalist society;

on the other hand, the opportunist error: it is true that in a socialist régime work has not yet become the individual's first requirement, and in consequence the direct and prime incentive to work is the interest of the workers in satisfying their material and cultural needs; this does not mean, however, that these needs are always of the same scope and nature and do not evolve historically.

The difficulty consists in being alive to the living dialectic of material incentives and moral incentives instead of setting them in opposition to one another: it is only by constantly orientating the material interests of individuals and collective works by means of a distribution according to the work done, and so guiding socialist commodity relationships towards the interests of society, that socialist morality is developed.

Historical experience has thus imposed the idea of a plurality of 'models' of this construction. The abolition of private ownership of the means of production, which is a first and essential condition for the social revolution of our day, is not in itself sufficient to do away with every form of man's alienation. Historical experience has shown that while a system of centralised planning, in the administration of collective ownership, can be absolutely necessary in certain historical conditions (particularly in the first stages of construction), at the same time it can produce technocratic and bureaucratic distortions in the concept of the State and even of the Party, and bring about new alienations of class in relation to Party and of Party and State in relation to the person of the administrator. On the other hand, while the transitory necessity of making very considerable allowance for the law of value and commodity relationships in a régime based on collective ownership of the means of production, and the system of 'auto-administration', make it possible to inaugurate a permanent 'auto-criticism', an immediate economic and political democracy, yet they come up against the problem of co-ordinating initiative from below and technical demands of national planning.

Whatever 'model' is used, according to the conditions proper to each nation, tension between the two demands still persists.

In this field, one can neither fall back on *spontaneity*, which would lead to an anarchical confrontation of group interests, nor on the *dogmatic claim* to determine from above the needs and appetites of the whole body of workers.

In the first case, we lost sight of *perspective*, in the second of *reality*.

The private interests of groups of producers cannot be reconciled with the general interests of society, unless one confronts the former with the interests of other workers who consume their products; and this cannot be done except through the medium of commodity relationships, of the law of value, and of prices.

Does this mean a return to the principles, in fact, of capitalism?

By no means: in the first place, in a socialist régime, the operation of the law of value is limited in its field of application.

The soil, for example, is in essence excluded from the circulation of commodities. Nevertheless there still remains in a socialist régime a distant equivalent of differential rent according to the quality of the soil, the climate, etc. In the immensely wealthy collective farms of Armenia and Georgia, the standard of living is very different from that of those in Siberia.

Labour, or rather labour-power, has ceased to be a commodity: nevertheless, the remuneration of the different categories of workers is not automatically determined by the quantity and quality of the work. It can vary appreciably according to circumstances and the need of the moment.

The very principle of planning is different in a socialist and a capitalist régime.

A conscious and deliberate control of the economy is not possible in a capitalist régime. At the most, certain forces can intervene to guide the economy not towards a single end, but towards a *number* of different ends, since it is the often divergent ends of large capitalist groups which direct investments; the 'plan' which is produced is the resultant of a relationship between antagonistic forces. In a socialist régime planning is not at the mercy of such cleavages, since it is determined not by a balance between competing appetites for profit but by the general needs of the whole of society.

This planning becomes increasingly difficult when socialism

has made it possible to provide for the immediate needs of the great masses. The plan is then no longer drawn beforehand in outline by the need to supply urgent necessities. When we reach a time when every citizen can be given three pairs of shoes a year, the target can no longer be the provision of six or a dozen pairs.

We then meet the problem of ends, and with it come problems of quality, of proportion, of balance and choice.

We can no longer believe blissfully in an 'objective law of harmonious development' in the sense in which Stalin meant it. Harmony has to be won in a day-to-day quest, and ends can no longer be determined exclusively from above.

Allowance must be made both for the real needs of the masses, effectively expressed in their lives, and for the economic possibilities that tend to allow more importance to questions of *profitability*. This in no way means a return to capitalist norms of profit, since in a socialist régime there is no possibility of private appropriation of surplus-value.

In a socialist régime, to take into account profitability is to ensure the continued accumulation of socialist resources, and to meet non-productive expenses (defence, social assistance, education, etc.).

Here again, commodity relationships and the operation of the law of value make it possible to determine profitability, to estimate socially necessary working hours, to overcome contradictions between the individual and the demands of society, between the short-term and the long-term, between the material incentive and the moral incentive.

Economic problems, then, and planning problems in particular, no longer appear in the same form as they did in the heroic era of the first five-year plans. Whether in the determination of ends or in that of methods of administration and harmonisation, they have become infinitely more complex.

This change in infrastructures calls for a change in superstructures.

For example, the fact of becoming alive to the objective

necessity of making allowance for commodity relationships over a long period, implies and requires a greater participation by the masses in the working out both of economic plans and of political decisions, in the administration of economic and political affairs. A new Soviet constitution is in course of preparation.

This situation raises new problems.

In philosophy it is not by chance that problems of humanism and alienation are assuming a central importance: they express the concern to make a break with all forms of positivism and scientism which lead to taking as an end what is only a means (whether it is a question of the system of planning and administration, of the form of the State or the structure of the Party).

In the human sciences Marxist sociology is developing more as an independent science, the more the necessity becomes apparent of concentrating more concretely on the study of the objective laws of socialist reality.

In political economy, new planning requirements have brought about the inclusion of studies that were formerly treated as 'bourgeois', such as econometrics and cybernetics.

In moral science, side by side with the values of discipline and sacrifice, emphasis is necessarily laid on the values of initiative and creation.

In aesthetics, it is no longer possible to maintain a polar contrast between socialist realism and critical realism, a contrast that derives from the complacent belief that socialism is already fully achieved, and that there is accordingly no longer any fundamental conflict between the individual and society, and no longer any alienation. A socialist realism which ceases to be critical founders in an idyllic irrealism.

This awareness of the great changes that have come about helps us to avoid a certain number of errors in the cultural field.

1. The error which consists in believing that, the economic and social conditions of socialism being realised, the super-

structures necessarily derive from them, and that man is going to be transformed automatically, as though he were no more than the product or resultant of the conditions in which he lives.

2. The error which consists in believing that culture is exclusively a means for achieving the short-term ends of an economic plan or a political project.

3. The error which consists in believing that science and technology can solve all the problems they raise, and in overlooking the humanist element in culture, which is the discovery of ends.

Such are the problems with which we are faced at the present stage in the growth of socialism.

*

The third great historic fact which profoundly transforms the very terms of the problem is that of the decolonisation, in less than twenty years, of two continents, Asia and Africa.

The fundamental historic significance of this new fact is that the West—that is, Europe and North America—is no longer the sole centre of historical initiative, the sole creator of values, of civilisation, and of culture.

Even if the people of Asia and the countries of black Africa have not created a technology as efficient as our own, it would be disastrous, for the humanism of our time, not to seek out and recognise the values created by peoples who were halted in their initial development and robbed of their own history by colonisation.

Marxism, which claims to be the heir of the whole culture of the past, cannot reduce this culture to the strictly western traditions of classical German philosophy, of English political economy, of French socialism, of Greek rationalism, of the technical spirit which emerged from the Renaissance.

Were it to do so, it would become purely western, and certain dimensions of man would elude it.

It is of the essence of its universal vocation to be rooted in the culture of every people. An Algerian, Islamic in culture, can arrive at scientific socialism by other roads than those of Hegel, Ricardo, or Saint-Simon. He has had his own Utopian socialism in the Carmathian movement, his rationalist and dialectical tradition in Averroes, his forerunner of historical materialism in Ibn Khaldun: and it is upon these traditions that he can graft scientific socialism. And this in no way excludes his integrating the heritage of our culture, *just as we have to integrate his*.

The reluctance to acknowledge kinship with materialism and to establish Marxist parties in black Africa, and the schism in Asia, are historical phenomena which raise fundamental problems.

It is not a question of denying or abandoning the rationalist and technical tradition in favour of the irrational, but of integrating all the forces of life in a rationalism that has been enriched by these contributions and, through knowledge of other fundamental attitudes to life, of obtaining the critical focus necessary to avoid dogmatising our own tradition.

Still less is it a question of accepting certain inverted racialisms which would result in stabilising peoples in their past.

What we have to do is to work out an authentically universal humanism, losing nothing that has been won by reason but ready to embrace new cultural areas.

By its very nature, Marxism is capable of this universality, and the rich experience of the battles for national freedom fought by hitherto colonised peoples and of the construction of socialism along roads proper to each one of them, will make a very considerable contribution to the richness of Marxism's own humanism.

If Marxism is not to become 'provincial', it cannot develop through monologue; it can do so only through dialogue with all man's creations.

The problems raised by decolonisation, in giving back their own history to formerly colonised peoples, guide us to a rediscovery of the living spirit of Marxism, beyond the schematisations and simplifications that are exploded by a wider exploration of the world.

*

Reflection on each of the three great facts of our century leads to one and the same conclusion.

The development of the sciences and technology has finally and permanently made obsolete the claim to possess once and for all either the prime elements of reality or the first principles of knowledge. As Bachelard emphasised, our modern method of knowledge is 'non-Cartesian': in every field it substitutes dialectic for intuition.

The development of socialism in different geographical and historical conditions, on the scale of several continents, imposes correspondingly the notion of a plurality of 'models', just as the universal process of decolonisation, by liberating new sources of human creation that have long been denied and held back by colonialism, forces us to widen the horizon of a humanism that has hitherto been regarded as exclusively western.

From whatever angle we approach the problems of the twentieth century, dogmatism has become untenable.

We must, therefore, start from a consideration of the nature of dogmatism.

CHAPTER TWO

From Dogmatism to Twentieth-Century Thought

*

The fantastic transformation of the world and the three great facts that characterise it have produced great confusion in philosophy.

No philosopher has yet succeeded, in these last twenty years, in mastering these new realities, in rising up to an over-all view comparable to the great syntheses of the Renaissance, from Leonardo da Vinci to Giordano Bruno and Descartes; or comparable to that of the eighteenth-century Encyclopaedists, to that of Marx a century ago, or of Lenin fifty years ago.

In this general philosophical confusion, why is it that Marxism can answer the questions which history and life raise for our times?

The reason is that with Marxism philosophy for the first time no longer claims to look down from a higher plane on things, on men and their history, but to be *the awareness and the driving force for action by which man transforms both things and himself, and builds his own history.*

Marxism, while including a factual experience which cannot be challenged by science because it is the very condition that makes science possible, is a philosophy which does not claim to constitute a complete and finished system, that is to say a system that must soon come into conflict with a reality that is constantly changing; for the system is always an image of the past, which alone is finished.

Marxist philosophy is the effort to make action transparent to thought and to forward thought by going beyond it.

Since its aim is to form one with the movement of things

and with man's action which transforms them, it is materialist and it is dialectical.

It is here that lies the essential superiority of the Marxist over other philosophies.

An essential superiority, because Marxism *can* provide the synthesis which our century needs, but has not yet done so.

It has created the economic and social conditions for a renaissance of culture infinitely finer than that of the earlier Renaissance. A culture, however, is not merely the resultant of the conditions that make it possible. New creative efforts are necessary to bring it up to the level of the needs and hopes that the very success of the Marxist revolutions has produced.

It is for Marxists to demonstrate the factual truth of this essential superiority and its practical reality at every new moment of history, by raising their philosophical, historical, moral and aesthetic consciousness to the level of the conditions they have themselves created. This was explicitly emphasised by Engels in his *Ludwig Feuerbach*: materialism must necessarily take a new form with every great discovery that marks a new epoch in the history of the sciences.

Since the time of Engels there have been many such epoch-making discoveries. To confine ourselves simply to the natural sciences, there have been quantum physics and relativity at the beginning of the century, and, in the middle of the century, cybernetics and, in biology, the synthesis and controlled modifications of nucleotids.

Can we say that Marxists have carried out Engels' programme?

On one occasion, in 1908, they did so, and in an exemplary way, with Lenin's *Materialism and Empirio-criticism*. Lenin spent three years in an intensive study of fundamental works on contemporary physics. Of English physicists, this included the works of Maxwell, Rücker, Ward, Pearson; of German, those of Ernst Mach, Hertz and Boltzmann, without counting the philosophical interpretations of Cohen and von Hartmann; of French, those of Henri Poincaré, Becquerel, Langevin, and the interpretations of Duhem and Le Roy, not to mention the speculations of the Russian revisionists.

If one had today to make a bibliography on this subject, stopping at 1908 (the date when Lenin wrote his book)—one would find that he had not left a single essential work unread. Starting from this scientific basis, he showed what could be the 'new form' of materialism corresponding to this stage of physics. He introduced a radically new theoretical idea, that of the inexhaustibility of matter. 'The electron is as inexhaustible as the atom.' This thesis entails philosophical consequences of capital importance, in particular that which forbids us to confuse with matter itself the *image* of matter which science constructs at a particular moment of its development.

That is without doubt the most fruitful conclusion that emerges from Lenin's book, his essential contribution to the fight against dogmatism in philosophy.

*

Marxism is not a pre-critical, dogmatic philosophy.

In philosophy, dogmatism is, historically, the opposite of *critique* in the sense which Kant first gave to the word, even though he did so in a context outside that of history. To simplify, we may say that the critical point of view in philosophy is the awareness of the fact that whatever we say about reality it is we who say it. Dogmatism, on the contrary, is the illusion or the claim of being entrenched in things and of pronouncing the absolute and definitive truth about them. The most typical example of dogmatism is religious dogmatism: its claim to teach, in the form of dogmas, absolute and definitive revealed truths. These are not human pronouncements, they are God's. They soar above men and their history.

There are, however, other forms of dogmatism; there are even materialist forms, such as those of the eighteenth-century French materialists, defining matter once and for all on the basis of the mechanistic concepts of Descartes, and from that starting point entrenching themselves in things in order to tell us the absolute truth about them.

Marxist materialism is by principle anti-dogmatic.

In his *Theses on Feuerbach* Marx already noted what was the chief defect in all forms of earlier materialism: that they did not see the *active element* of knowledge, the act by which man, in order to know things, first goes out to meet them, projecting schemata by which to perceive them and hypotheses by which to conceive them, and then verifies *in practice* the correctness of his schemata, his hypotheses, his models. Knowledge is a *construction* of 'models' and the only criterion of their value is practice.

Marx, Engels, and Lenin attached such importance to this active element of knowledge worked out by Kant, Fichte and Hegel that, materialists though they were, they always maintained that the basic philosophic source of Marxist philosophy is precisely German idealism: German *idealism*, let me emphasise, because although Feuerbach must be included in German philosophy it is not he who is cited as the basic source. Engels continually insists in his *Ludwig Feuerbach* that Feuerbach is 'infinitely poorer' than Hegel: in his preface, in 1874, to his *Peasants' War* he declares that 'without German philosophy, particularly that of Hegel, scientific socialism . . . would never have come into existence' (trans. M. J. Olgin, London, 1927, p. 27). Again, in 1891, he says, 'We German socialists are proud of having as our origin not only Saint-Simon, Fourier and Owen, but also Kant, Fichte and Hegel.'

All dogmatic interpretations of Marxism begin by underestimating the legacy of those three philosophers and going back to Feuerbach, to Diderot or to Spinoza.

To recognise this heritage of German idealism in no way implies a belittling of the materialist element in Marx's thought. All it does is to rule out any confusion with pre-Marxist, dogmatic and speculative, forms of materialism.

It is precisely because Marxism has abandoned the speculative and dogmatic claim of being a philosophy moving on a higher level than the sciences and exempt from their vicissitudes that it has become a science.

Marxist materialism is a recall to a more modest attitude: by affirming that the world exists outside my own self and without me, and that it has no need of me in order to exist, but at the same time by never confusing this world with the model of it, sometimes more complex, sometimes less, which science constructs at each epoch of history, dialectical materialism is conscious of the fact that the real is inexhaustible, is irreducible to the knowledge we have of it, and that every scientific concept is always a provisional construction, pending the appearance of richer, more effective and truer constructions.

Marxist materialism—a critical philosophy in as much as it never forgets that everything I say about things is said by a man and not by a God—bars us, as materialism, from the idealist illusion of confusing, as Hegel did, our conceptual reproduction of the world in models that are always approximate, with its production. This idealist illusion persists obstinately: Bachelard said that every scientific fact is a cluster of concepts, and that is true enough so long as one does not forget that the converse is not true. I cannot reconstitute objective reality from clusters of concepts organised in accordance with the laws of logical coherence or harmony. Reality is neither reducible to mathematics, as Descartes thought, nor to aesthetics, as Leibniz suggested.

The materialist element of knowledge, according to Marx and Lenin, is governed by the criterion of the practical, that of experimental verification of our hypotheses, our models; for that alone can ultimately guarantee that our conceptual construction corresponds to an objective reality. As Marx wrote in his second thesis on Feuerbach, 'The question whether objective truth is an attribute of human thought is not a theoretical but a practical question. Man must prove the truth, i.e. the reality and power, the "this-sidedness" (*Diesseitigkeit*), of his thinking in practice' (*The German Ideology*, p. 197).

This dialectical materialism is distinguished from all earlier forms of materialism in particular by the fact that it takes into account dialectical relationships between relative truths and absolute truths.

For a Marxist every truth is at the same time a relative truth and an absolute truth.

Every scientific theory which accounts for phenomena within its province is a relative truth in this sense, that it will sooner or later be supplanted by a more comprehensive and wider theory which will include it and reduce it to being only one particular instance of a more general truth. At the same time it is an absolute truth in the sense that the theory which supplants it will necessarily include all that the earlier theory explains and which it allows us to grasp.

This 'relativity', as Lenin emphasised in *Materialism and Empirio-criticism*, is far from leading to relativism: for every scientific discovery and every theory which accounts for it constitute a definitive acquisition for science, and one that cannot again be challenged, since it has given us for all time an effective power in the handling of nature and in consequence an at any rate approximate reflection of its reality.

This dialectic of relationships between relative and absolute truth plays a leading role, for, if we are not to give a false (and fatalistic) idea of scientific socialism, we must have a clear idea of what a scientific truth is, and we must not believe that the only way to escape scepticism and eclecticism is to take refuge in a dogmatic rationalism which opposes ideology and science in the same way as the Cartesians opposed truth and error. It is to stand outside the real line of advance in the sciences to think that we can once and for all establish ourselves in the concept, possess first principles, immutable and complete, and henceforth progress from concept to concept.

There does exist a kernel of absolute truth won by science, which cannot be challenged; but of this kernel of absolute truth (that is, the sum total of the real powers of which we dispose, and the resemblance which that entails between the scientific models we have constructed and reality) we must say:

1. That it is never complete.

2. That it is present within concepts, theories, models, which are constantly subject to revision and constantly relative.

Scientific socialism, as its name indicates, lays claim to the same type of truth as science itself. It is a science and, like every science,

1. It contains a kernel of absolute truth in the sense that it enables us to grasp the phenomena it studies, the phenomena of history, and that this mastery entails a certain resemblance between the theory and the level of reality of which it is the theory.

2. This kernel of absolute truth is undergoing continual growth.

3. This growth is not produced by mechanical addition, but by an organic development which at each stage calls for an overall reorganisation of concepts.

To confer on Marxism the prerogative of an 'absolutely absolute' truth (which would not be *at the same time* both relative and absolute), to allow it to be free from the vicissitudes of scientific progress, would be to rob it of its character as a science and give it the immutability of a dogma; for the characteristic proper to religious dogmatism is that it rules out the dialectic of absolute and relative truth. Marxism cannot at the same time class itself as a science and claim a status of truth that could only be absolute, the (illusory) status of metaphysics and theology.

As an illustration of this idea, let us take a simple example: the materialist theory of reflection in knowledge.

Lucretius presented it in a primitive form: particles of matter, atoms, are emitted by the object. Their impact on this other aggregation of atoms which constitutes ourselves, produces in us a reflection of those things and so gives birth to knowledge. Naïve though it is, this 'model' nevertheless contains a kernel of absolute truth: there can be no reflection without an object that is reflected. There we have one of the foundations of materialism. One could say as much of the materialism which emerged from English empiricism or eighteenth-century France.

Nevertheless, it is a relative truth, since the dialectical materialism of Marx, integrating the rich contribution of the German idealist tradition on the 'active side of knowledge', makes it clear that the reflection is not present initially. It is formed in a succession of approximations, by means of hypotheses which are constructed by a man who acts, and are invalidated or confirmed by practice. This richer concept, however, preserves and renders more fruitful the kernel of absolute truth in the earlier materialism: the priority of the thing to consciousness, a definitive acquisition, and one that cannot be challenged by science since it is the condition that makes science possible.

Thus it remains true that knowledge is, *by its nature*, a *reflection*, in the sense that it is the knowledge of a reality which is not our own work, and that it is at the same time, *by its method*, a *'construction'*.

The notion of 'model' allows us to retain the two essential elements of the Marxist theory of knowledge: the materialist element of the reflection which saves us from the idealist, Hegelian, illusion which confuses the conceptual reconstruction of reality with its construction, and the *active* element, the element of construction, which saves us from the dogmatic illusion which confuses this provisional model with an absolute and complete truth.

*

All the errors that have been made in philosophical discussion of the sciences during the last twenty-five years arise from a dogmatic failure to recognise this dialectic of relative truth and absolute truth; and this applies as much to the concept of materialism as it does to that of dialectic or of historical materialism.

For example, if we accept as absolute and complete truth the form assumed by materialism at one moment in its history, in virtue of a certain image of matter that science presents, then, as soon as science modifies that image we shall be obliged, as Lenin showed in his *Materialism and Empirio-criticism*, either to challenge materialism itself, by speaking of a 'vanishing of matter', simply because the new image does not correspond with the earlier; or to reject as idealist a physical or chemical theory on the ground that the new image it presents of matter or of determinism does not correspond with the earlier.

The same error can be made with dialectics. If we take as absolute and complete truth a certain number of laws of dialectics which are in fact at each period the balance sheet, always provisional, of what has been won by reason—an absolute truth, that is, as a balance sheet of conquests in the past, but a relative truth as an introduction to conquests still to come—and if we claim to judge the truth or falsity of a scientific theory by its agreement or non-agreement with the already known laws of dialectics (as has happened with biology in particular), then a Marxism conceived in this way cannot carry out its emancipating and fructifying role but becomes a brake on research.

The same error can be made with historical materialism: if we take as absolute and complete truth the scheme of the five stages of historical development which has been constructed on the basis of our experience of the development of western societies, and if we seek at all costs to include in this scheme the development of African or Asian societies, for example, then we leave behind scientific methods and return to a speculative and dogmatic philosophy of history; moreover, we mutilate the thought of Marx, who had raised this problem in connexion with the 'asiatic method of production'. Marx and Engels were already writing with reference to these five stages: 'Viewed apart from real history, these abstractions have in themselves no value whatsoever. They can only serve to facilitate the arrangement of historical material . . . but they by no means afford a recipe or schema, as does philosophy, for neatly trimming the epochs of history' (*The German Ideology*, pp. 38-9).

Marxism is a scientific concept of the world, and as such, it is an instrument of scientific research: not in the sense that it will allow us, on the ground of philosophical principles, to forestall scientific experiment, except as a mere working hypothesis or hypothetical basis for research, but precisely in this sense, that on principle it puts us on our guard against the dogmatism of every theory which claims to be exclusive and definitive.

The opposite of dogmatism is the recognition of the necessity for a plurality of scientific hypotheses: subject to the condition that this *pluralism* is not understood in a metaphysical or relativist sense.

To give it a metaphysical sense would be to consider it outside of history, that is as a definitive, unsurpassable limit; and this would lead to scepticism and relativatism by recognising as an inevitable necessity a number of irreducible truths and in consequence no truth at all; while valid pluralism, as the driving force in scientific development, is a factor that is constantly provisional but constantly superseded and constantly reborn. Pluralism constantly requires a synthesis, but this synthesis, in its turn, is seen to be not a final term but a stage starting from which a new pluralism is born, which again will call for a new synthesis, and so on.

To give pluralism a relativist sense would be to place on the same footing all the working hypotheses that confront one another: whereas at every moment one of them is finally seen to be capable of integrating and going beyond all the others.

It is this that distinguishes dialectical from 'sophistical' reasoning.

Sophistics confines itself to an abstract view, to a single aspect of the movement of thought, by asserting that in every error there is some portion of truth, without seeking, or being able to distinguish the importance of that portion. By contrast, while dialectics involves the necessity of a critical assimilation, of an integration of all the partial truths found in the pluralism of hypotheses, it calls for an effort to overcome it: the truest hypothesis being ultimately that which is seen to be capable of integrating all the others.

It is important, however, to remember:

1. That it is not a privilege which can be accorded *a priori* from a starting point in past certainties; it must be won in practice.

2. That it never constitutes a definitive victory upon which one can rest permanently.

*

Socialism does not become scientific simply by a transition from idealism to materialism, but by a transition from speculation to criticism, from Utopianism to the experimental method.

A materialism can perfectly well be speculative, as were the speculations of Lucretius about atoms, or those of Descartes on the application of mechanics to biology, or, nearer our own time, those of Stalin when he used philosophical materialism not as a science capable of guiding action but as an ideology to justify a policy. Materialist metaphysics has no more value than idealist metaphysics.

In his *Socialism: Utopian and Scientific*, Engels rejected 'the concept of nature which prevailed as much in the French of the eighteenth century as in the work of Hegel' (cf. *Selected Works*, p. 415).

Whether in socialism, in philosophy or in history, the scientific attitude calls in the first place for an end to the myth of absolute knowledge (expressed in its final perfected form by Hegel), and thereby the end, too, of the illusion of a philosophy moving at a higher level than the sciences and immune from their vicissitudes.

'Ideology' (in the pejorative sense of the word—and Marx, Engels and Lenin do not use it always in such a sense but often as a synonym for 'theory') in so far as it contrasts with scientific theory, is characterised not necessarily as error in relation to truth, as opinion in relation to concept, as an inverted image of the real in relation to a true image, but primarily by the fact that it is unaware of its own origins and relativity. The ideological illusion consists in forgetting that every ideology, like every theory, is born of a *practice*, and that it is born *in history*. There is no absolute knowing in which knowledge is equivalent to and identical with the being it knows. Knowledge is a representation or a reconstruction that aims at accounting for the real. This reconstruction is always a function of the degree of man's development, of the techniques, the practice and the concepts, always provisional, which man has evolved. It is an ideological illusion to take the reconstruction as an absolute and definitive truth whose principles cannot be challenged again.

Ideologies can accordingly contain extremely important elements of truth; sometimes they can even contain 'stupendously grand thoughts and germs of thought that everywhere break through their fantastic covering' (*Socialism: Utopian and Scientific* in *Selected Works*, p. 403).

One may quote, as examples of such ideologies, the socialist Utopias which, as Engels explains, are, like scientific socialism, 'the direct product of the recognition, on the one hand, of the class antagonisms existing in the society of today between proprietors and non-proprietors, between capitalists and wage-workers; on the other hand, of the anarchy existing in production' (*Ibid*, p. 399). This ideology is in no way an inverted or false reflection of reality. But, Engels adds, 'Like every new theory, modern socialism had, at first, to connect itself with the intellectual stock-in-trade ready to its hand, however deeply its roots lay in material economic facts,' so that, 'in its theoretical form, modern socialism originally appears ostensibly as a more logical extension of the principles laid down by the great French philosophers of the eighteenth century . . . The French philosophers of the eighteenth century, the forerunners of the Revolution, appealed to reason as the sole judge of all that is. A rational government, rational society, were to be founded . . . We have seen that this eternal reason was in reality nothing but the idealised understanding of the eighteenth-century citizen, just then evolving into the bourgeois'. But this historical illusion 'also dominated the founders of socialism. To the crude conditions of capitalist production and the crude class conditions corresponded crude theories. The solution of the social problems, which as yet lay hidden in undeveloped economic conditions, the Utopians attempted to evolve out of the human brain. Society presented nothing but wrongs; to remove these was the task of reason' (*Ibid*, pp. 399-403).

Engels recalls that at earlier stages this demand for a new society, rooted in the contradictions of nascent capitalism, was attached not to 'reason' but to religious faith; we find this, for example, in Thomas Münzer at the time of the Reformation and the Peasants' War or, at the time of the English Revolution, in the Levellers.

Engels was far from dismissing, with lordly disdain, this ideological heritage, far from establishing a radical, metaphysical, opposition between ideology and science (he left that to the 'literary small-fry' and 'philistines' who 'crow over the superiority of their own bald reasoning as compared with such "insanity" ', *Ibid*, p. 403)—on the contrary, he adopted a truly scientific attitude towards them. In these forerunners he looks above all for the truths they contribute, removing from them the strictly ideological illusion that 'socialism is the expression of absolute truth, reason and justice . . . independent of time, space and the historical development of man' (*Ibid*, p. 409), a truth that is the fruit of a divine revelation or an immutable reason. This pre-critical belief is characteristic of dogmatic rationalism: the Platonic theory of 'ideas' of which dogmatic Marxism constitutes a naturalist variant, or Spinozism, of which it is a dynamic variant, simply substituting 'matter in movement' for Spinoza's 'substance' but retaining the pre-critical illusion of being able to rise to concepts which are rigorously and definitively equated with reality.

'To make a science of socialism, it had first to be placed on a real basis' (*Ibid*, p. 410). 'Its task was no longer to manufacture a system of society as perfect as possible, but to examine the historico-economic succession of events from which these classes and their antagonism had necessarily sprung, and to discover in the economic conditions thus created the means of ending the conflict' (*Ibid*, p. 416).

From that starting point Engels recalls how Marx solved this problem by 'two great discoveries, the materialist conception of history and the revelation of the secret of capitalistic production through *surplus value* . . . With these discoveries socialism became a science. The next thing was to work out all its details and relations' (*Ibid*).

In that we have a remarkable definition of the conditions in which there is a transition from speculative, utopian, ideology to a 'socialist ideology' which has become scientific theory through criticism of 'ideological illusions': *historical materialism* makes it possible to get rid of the illusion of the transcendence of revelation or reason, the illusion that 'history must always be written according to an extraneous standard' (*The German Ideology*, p. 51). 'Men are the producers of their conceptions, ideas, etc.—real, active men, as they are. conditioned by a definite development of their productive forces and of the intercourse corresponding to these' (*Ibid*,

p. 37). Thus reason is re-integrated, as an historical creation of man, in the strict immanence of global social practice. This transition from speculation to materialist criticism or critical materialism is the first condition of a scientific thought.

The second condition is the transition from utopianism to experimental method. Engels emphasises the importance in this connexion of the discovery of *surplus value* as the fundamental concept which accounts for what is specific to the method of capitalist production. Socialism is not the utopian construction of an 'ideal' social system. 'Communism is not . . . an ideal to which reality will have to adjust itself. We call communism the real movement which abolishes the present state of things' (*Ibid*, p. 48).

The whole of Marx's works forbids us to give these expressions a positivist interpretation.

The positivist interpretation is that which consists in dealing with this 'real movement' without bearing in mind the specific character of human history in relation to the development of physical nature or to animal evolution. It consists in forgetting, in short, that it is men who have been making their own history ever since they invented the tool and, by their labour, have transformed themselves in transforming nature. Since that time, as Marx emphasised in the passage from *Capital* already quoted, their projects precede their acts and impose themselves on them as their law. Even if these projects and these acts are alienated, even if 'what each individual wants is hindered by each other individual and what emerges is something that nobody wanted' (as Engels wrote to Joseph Bloch on 21st September 1890, thus likening the movement of history right up to our own days to a movement of nature)—even so it is none the less true (letter of 25th January 1894 to Heinz Starkenburg) that 'men make their history *themselves*, but *until now* they have not conformed to a collective will, to an overall plan . . . their efforts run counter to one another, and that is precisely the reason why, in all societies of this sort, *necessity*, completed and made manifest by chance, is paramount.'

*

The primacy of practice and the critical and active concept of knowledge enable us to set in its correct perspective the problem of the nature of dialectic and of the dialectic of nature.

The question has often been asked: how can a critical philosophy, without contradicting itself, admit a dialectic of nature?

The fundamental error of pre-Marxist, pre-critical, materialism is its dogmatism. By its neglect of the *active* character of knowledge, this has always led it to regarding as a structure of nature 'in itself' what was merely the image that we are able to construct of it, using, at each stage of development of the sciences and technology, the materials and concepts at our disposal. Materialism asserts that nature exists independently of ourselves and without ourselves, but that science does not.

The theory of knowledge in all non-critical, non-Marxist, materialism is based on a mechanistic concept of the reflection; that is to say it places the reflection at the starting point of knowledge, as though knowledge were the passive acceptance of the 'data' provided by a nature in itself, whereas knowledge is at the same time both *reflection* in as much as it is science already formed, and *projection* in as much as it is science in process of formation. Reflection—that is a reproduction or representation, more correct or less correct, of what actually happens in nature—is not a starting point (as the English empiricists or the eighteenth-century French materialists believed) but the fruit of a lengthy work of construction of successive 'projects', 'models', hypotheses, by which we actively challenge things, accepting the denials they force upon us and then changing the initial hypothesis and completely reorganising our whole body of knowledge (as Newton did in rejecting Ptolemy's representation, or Einstein in abandoning the physical system of Newton and even the geometry of Euclid).

In other words, it is by an illegitimate assimilation that one passes from the materialist affirmation of the priority of nature to the dogmatic affirmation of the pre-existence in nature, in the form in which they are present in our minds, of laws or categories, of concepts or structures which represent in our thought the fruit of a lengthy construction, of a long historical elaboration and of a frequent challenging.

For the last quarter of a century, unfortunately, interpretation of Engel's *Dialectics of Nature* has been vitiated by this pre-Marxist concept. Instead of seeing in this rich collection of notes a reflection by Engels on the science of his time, which sought to bring out the overall picture of nature which seemed to derive from the study of the most general laws of nature, of society, and of thought, as they appeared *in the science of this epoch*, a claim has been made (notably in Stalin's regrettably well-known compendium *Dialectical Materialism and Historical Materialism*) to extract from it an exhaustive catalogue of 'laws' or 'characteristics' of a dialectic which are universally and absolutely valid.

As we have already seen, the starting point of thought is never the bare noting of a prime datum. From the very beginning it is an act, the production of a 'model' or overall hypothesis, and thereby it includes some element of myth.

It is by this extraction from the datum, by this detachment from the immediate, that the movement of thought begins, by way of myth. Henri Wallon has shown that primitive man constituted the detour through the social which is the prelude to the birth of concept in order to act upon the real, and so rationalise it.

Thought, initially mythical and ritual, was later to become technique and science, and between myth and science there is not only continuity of function but divergence of method and opposition. Myth is the past of science, since myth does not, as does scientific hypothesis, submit itself to the criterion of practice.

Kant noted the difference between two uses of reason: that which submits to experimental verification, and that which claims to be emancipated from it and to operate outside all experiment. Kant gave the name of *dialectic* to precisely this speculative use, non-experimental and non-scientific, of reason.

For Kant, dialectic was the contradiction between two ideas, such as those of finite and infinite, freedom and necessity, etc. Dialectic unfolded exclusively within the subject.

Should we say no more than that dialectic lies, on the contrary, in the encounter between the subject and what it comes up against, and define it as subject-object relationship? This would be to assert that only the relationship between man and nature is dialectical. There can be no doubt but that this relationship is indeed dialectical, but we can go further.

Dialectic begins with this 'splitting of the one' by which, as Wallon has shown, in the very rise of primitive myth, thought creates a first cleavage between the world of immediate appearance and that of underlying reality conceived in the form of myth.

A second contradiction arises when thought, abandoning the transcendent illusions of myth, recognises that it is no more than a hypothesis, and in consequence accepts confrontation with reality by submitting to the verdict of practice. If the 'model' it constructs does not 'hold', if, that is, it does not account for the phenomena and allow us to grasp them, to handle them, then we shall have either to make the model more complex or to replace it by moving on to a complete reorganisation of our knowledge. Contradiction and totality are therefore two inseparable moments in this dialectic of knowledge, which is at the same time a dialectic of work, being a particular instance of the latter.

The characteristic proper to dialectical reason is therefore that it proceeds from totalisation to totalisation, from one provisional totalisation to another provisional totalisation, the transition from one to the other being called for by the resistance, the check, the contradiction of the real in relation to the earlier totalisation.

The role of dialectical reason in history is relatively easy to determine, because history is ultimately the sum of what men have made, and in consequence the first dialectic of work can be rediscovered in it. Marx's *Capital* provides an outstanding example of this dialectic. Instead of stopping short, as though at ultimate truths, at what is only a human product, Marx finds in the production of commodities, for example, not a datum of nature but a product of culture, a fundamental human relationship. This enables him to get rid of the positivism of classical political economy, that is to get back, beyond 'given' objects, to the human activity that created them. In a more general way, as Marx explains in his chapter on 'the fetishism of commodities', this method makes it possible to proceed from the phenomenon to the essence; to consider, for example, economic realities not as things, as 'natural' realities existing from all eternity outside man and without man, but as beings created by man, whether it is a matter of products or of institutions. Thus the dialectic of *Capital* becomes a dialectic of work.

The economy ceases then to be seen as a phenomenon of nature from which man is absent, a phenomenon which will gradually govern the whole development of politics, of culture, and of history in general.

The economy is one, primordial, aspect of men's relationship with nature. In the organic totality of relationships, from which are born technology, science, philosophy, religion and the arts, the economy plays a decisive part; even so it never constitutes the sole driving force, after which everything else is epiphenomenon.

The historical materialism of Marx, accordingly, is a method neither of deduction nor of reduction. The superstructures cannot be deduced from the base, nor can they be reduced to it. All one can say is that both superstructures and base are elements of one and the same organic whole, in which the relationships of society (regarded as a system or living whole), together with the natural context which embraces it, play a major part.

We can now bring out certain characteristics of dialectical reason which distinguish it from the reason of traditional rationalism.

1. Dialectical reason is in the first place *reason that is in process of being formed,* as opposed to an already constituted rationality with its immutable laws, like those of formal logic. Adapting a well-known phrase, we may say that henceforth we know that logics are mortal.

From the Aristotelian logic of inclusion and immobile being, we have moved on to the logics of relation and movement, from the logic of identity to that of contradiction, from the logic of substance and attributes to that of life.

2. Dialectical reason is as much the art of formulating *questions* as it is the method of finding an *answer* to them. For if the real is not an immutable datum but a world in constant genesis, the reason that endeavours to create models in its likeness is forced once again to challenge its principles in order at every moment to formulate the problems in terms that correspond to the new situation. Reason has a history. This history is not the history of successive answers given to one and the same question, but the history of complete recastings of the very formulation of the question.

3. Dialectical reason is distinct both from the classical rationalism of the seventeenth and eighteenth centuries, and from the lesser rationalism of the end of the nineteenth and beginning of the twentieth centuries. The classical rationalism of Descartes, Spinoza, of Leibniz and even of Diderot held that reason, by itself alone, could determine the *ends* of our action. Lesser rationalism, the rationalism of positivism and scientism, reduced reason to being no more than a cal-

culation of the *means* for attaining a given end. From Auguste Comte to Durkheim and Lévy-Bruhl's *Ethics and Moral Science*, the positivist reason of this lesser rationalism, in evading philosophical problems by a sort of intellectual trickery, can only give the illusion of being able to direct action by assigning ends for it. Positivism is inseparable from agnosticism and opens the road to pure fideism. Starting from the correct idea that there are no final ends, this positivism concludes that there are no ends at all and that, in consequence, there is no philosophical method for determining them.

Dialectical reason does not admit, with classical rationalism, that reason takes the place of decision, nor with lesser rationalism, that it authorises an arbitrary choice.

What characterises dialectical reason is that it combines a reason which guides action without determining it, and a responsible decision, at once rational and free, which goes beyond, without destroying, constituted reason. Reason is not a transcendent order but the continued creation of a human order.

4. Dialectical reason is an element in the rational construction of reality. It is not contemplation, but construction, of an order. The element of negativity, that of the rejection of the already constituted order, of the rejection of the illusion of a world already fully made outside ourselves and without ourselves, is an essential element: it is the element by which the increasing unity of the history of nature and of man is affirmed.

The rational, it has been said, is increasingly the operational.

For, if nature is humanised, man is an initially natural being and, consequently, the agreement of his thought with the nature from which he emerged and from which his very thought was born, is neither a mystery nor a miracle. Man, in one and the same movement, thinks reality and realises his thought.

Here, however, we meet a problem: how is this dialectical reason itself constituted? Man's thought has been obliged to become dialectical only in order to integrate with reality aspects of nature that are impatient of any other logic. The primacy of practice asserts itself once again as the criterion of the truth of thought and its at least approximate equation with the real.

Dialectic is not an *a priori* scheme that one superimposes on things and thrusts upon them by forcing them into this Procrustean bed. The laws of dialectic are not a closed system of thought like the logical forms of Aristotle, the categories of Kant or the logic of Hegel. The very principles of Marxism call for a study of the laws of dialectic, not as defining the immutable structure of an absolute Reason, but, let me repeat, as a balance sheet, always provisional, of the victories of rationality, drawn up for each great historical epoch.

From this critical point of view, we may speak of a dialectic of nature, but not in a dogmatic sense that would entail arbitrary belief in the possibility of an absolute spectator, outside history.

We may speak of a dialectic of nature, for I cannot confine myself to the affirmation of the bare existence of an original nature, as do agnostics or pragmatists.

Materiality is not simply negation, limit, check, or resistance in relation to the act of thought or of human practice.

For this negation is not unspecified, anonymous, abstract, always identical with itself: the 'in-self' (*an sich*) answers 'No' to such an hypothesis. Sometimes, too, it answers 'Yes'. This answer has a *practical* character: nature either allows itself to be handled, or refuses. By acting according to one particular hypothesis my action miscarries; by acting according to another I have power over nature. It is true that the hypotheses destroy themselves and that none of them can claim to disclose an ultimate structure of being. But every dead hypothesis, simply because it has been alive, bequeaths to us a new power over nature. This power and this knowledge

59

have survived it. The new hypothesis is the heir of the hypothesis it replaces and has destroyed. These powers, accordingly, have accumulated, and my acts of today, making use of them in order to handle nature, carve out at any rate a rough model of its structure, which is known to me in ever greater detail.

The history of the sciences teaches us that the demands of the object have in turn exploded and rendered useless the principles of the mechanics of Descartes, Newton and Laplace, the laws of logic of Aristotle and Kant, and Euclid's principles of geometry.

From physics to biology, the natural sciences have continually exerted an increasing pressure on our habits of thought.

They have obliged those who investigate such matters to invent other models than those of traditional logic, of Euclidean geometry, of classical mechanics.

Now, if a hypothesis to explain structure is confirmed, if it is shown to be effective, if it enables us to grasp things and allows us even to discover new properties in them, how can we conceive that there is no relationship (I do not say a relationship of identity) between the concept and the 'in-self' which it has in view?

How could a dialectical thought allow us to grasp a being that is in no degree dialectical?

To speak of a dialectic of nature involves no arbitrary, dogmatic (that is, pre-critical) extrapolation of knowledge to being.

To say that there is a dialectic of nature is not to claim to know in advance, and *ne varietur*, the fundamental laws of the development of nature; on the contrary, it is, under the irresistible pressure of scientific discoveries, to see in Aristotelian logic, in the assumptions of Euclid, or in the principles of classical mechanics, no more than one particular case or one moment of rationality, within a much more general and constantly changing dialectical rationality.

To say that there is a dialectic of nature, is to say that the structure and the movement of reality are such that only a dialectical thought can make phenomena intelligible and allow us to handle them.

That is no more than an inference: but it is an inference founded on the totality of human practice—an inference that is constantly subject to revision as a function of the progress of that practice.

In that we have the fundamental characteristics of every scientific inference.

It presents itself not as a dogma but as a working hypothesis.

At the current stage of the development of the sciences, the representation of the real which emerges from the sum total of confirmed knowledge, is that of an organic whole in constant process not only of development but also of auto-creation. It is this structure that we call 'dialectical' as opposed to the mechanistic, metaphysical, concepts which would look on the world as an accumulation of isolated, abstract, elements whose form and movement are external to the matter to which they apply, and in which nothing new appears apart from a new arrangement of the pre-existing elements.

This concept of the world in which Marx saw a kinship with that of Jakob Boehme, in virtue of the latter's qualitative view of movement, which Lenin found akin to that of Heraclitus, and of which cybernetics today offers us a new and more accurate version by in some way expressing in mathematical terms the analogy of the forms of movement with the different levels of reality—this concept can serve as a working hypothesis and play an illuminating part in research.

From this point of view, cybernetics and the theory of information provide the notion of the dialectic of nature with the most striking theoretical and practical confirmation that any scientific concept has ever received a century after its formulation.

*

61

The Marxist concept of materialism and dialectic can today integrate everything that in the thought of the twentieth century has transformed the notions of the real, of truth, of beauty or of morality.

Traditionally, truth—like beauty, too, and morality—used to be defined by the conformity of our actions to an 'order', in the threefold sense of law, of harmony or of command.

In our day, the 'active', constructive, creative element which Marx emphasised, is taking on a new value.

In our scientific representation of the world it is becoming, we find, more and more difficult, and will ultimately be impossible, radically to separate in the object what the thing would be 'in itself' without us, and the knowledge we have of it; in other words, to isolate the 'thing' from the totality of technical or conceptual operations by which we think and experience it. This in no way entails the idealist landslide at the end of which we would see no more in the object than a construction of our own mind. It is only a question of our consciously realising this situation: at the present stage of the sciences we cannot isolate as two terms confronting one another the constructed reflection and the objective fact, as we would separate a cake from the baking-tin. Scientific laws are not a copy of an archetypal reason, like Plato's *ideas*, nor a copy of absolute laws of a nature-in-itself whose primordial legislator is some God or other. Scientific laws are not a copy of anything; they are constructions of our mind, always approximate and provisional, which allow us to take hold of a reality which we have not created, and of which only practice, methodical experiment, can guarantee us that our models correspond in some degree to its structure, that from a certain point of view they are at least 'isomorphous'.

What is challenged by the present development of the sciences is not 'the thing in itself'; it is the traditionally dogmatic concept of that 'thing in itself'. This concept is dogmatic when it confuses 'the thing in itself' with the representation of matter which science gives us at this stage or that stage of its development, when it takes as absolute and definitive truth what is no more than an approximate and provisional model.

Paul Ricoeur, in an attack on a dogmatic concept of transcendence from above, writes with great force (*De l'Interpretation*, p. 159) that 'religion is the reification and alienation of faith.' Defining 'the horizon' as 'the metaphor of what comes closer without ever becoming an object possessed,' he shows that 'the idol is the reification of the horizon into thing' (p. 510).

Transposing his demonstration on dialectical theology from transcendence from above (the transcendence of a God endowed with immutable characteristics, an anthropomorphic and finite God) to 'transcendence from below' (the transcendence which postulates a matter defined from ultimate elements and eternal laws), I would not hesitate to say that dogmatism in philosophy begins when 'horizon-function' declines into 'object-function'. Scientism is the reification and alienation of science: it substitutes the claim to absolute knowledge for dialectical reason which conceives 'the thing in itself' as the horizon of my aims and constructions.

Contemporary arts give us a direct awareness of this inversion of attitude in our concept of nature: neither picture nor novel sets out to reproduce by the methods of traditional realism, either a nature made nature or a nature becoming nature, whose formal norms, whose 'canons' or 'golden numbers' we would *re*-discover. The artist strives, on the contrary, to find a language which can suggest to us that the world is always in process of being made, with man's participation, in a living dialectic in which the project and the 'given object' mutually, to borrow a word from Van Lier, 'auto-regulate' one another.

The challenge to classical perspective and to a space traditionally, from Euclid to Newton, from Apelles to Raphael, held to be 'natural' and immutable, a challenge expressed in a movement which, from Cézanne to cubism, becomes increasingly self-conscious, brings out the part played by human initiative and construction in what used to be taken as a factual 'datum'. It is the same with the novelist's time, whose earlier postulates of linear continuity and irreversibility are challenged in the latest writings of Aragon as they are in the 'new novel'.

The same remarks would hold good for ethics, which is less and less seen as observation and observance of rules, and more and more as invention of these rules: not in a Nietzschean arbitrary decision nor in a Gide-like nihilism, but in a rigorous discipline of construction and creation as demanding as that of the arts—and this, too, in the continuation and supersession of a history.

The second distinguishing characteristic of this modern humanism, in comparison with the old, is *pluralism*. This too derives from the new concept of the real. Bachelard had already characterised the contemporary theory of knowledge of quanta and relativity as 'non-Cartesian', in the sense that it has abandoned the attempt to discover 'prime elements' whether in nature (as for example the 'indivisible' atoms of Democritus), or in thought (as for example in the concepts of Aristotle or the 'simple natures' of Descartes).

Thereby, too, is ruled out the claim to proceed by way of univocal deduction starting from first principles, and so rejoin, at the level of ultimate consequences, a 'concrete' which has become completely transparent to thought.[1]

Finally, there is an end to the ambition to grasp the real as a closed totality, in a network of concepts that constitutes a finished system. Neither the geometry nor the mechanist

[1] This of course in no way rules out the possibility, and even the necessity, of the element of *constructive deduction*, which is a capital element in scientific thought, provided it be conceived critically (as deductive mental construction) and not dogmatically (as participation in an essence of the real).

physics of Laplace, nor the Newtonian heavens—and this applies equally, moreover, to the political economy of Adam Smith, to the atomist psychology or mechanist history of Taine, or the sociology of Auguste Comte, and of Durkheim —none of these has been able to stand up to the test of a rapidly accelerating development of the natural and human sciences which are exposing the relative, historical character of their methodological postulates.

Scientific progress is effected not from a starting point in immutable principles, to arrive ultimately, through linear deductions, at a complete systematic totality, but by the way of overall, all-embracing, reorganisations of the conceptual field.

It may happen that different, partial, aspects of reality are arrived at by starting from different, even indeed from contrary, hypotheses, and by the construction of different 'models'. That is why 'pluralism' of scientific and artistic schools is a first condition of a healthy development of the sciences and arts.

In this context, pluralism in no way leads to scepticism or eclecticism, any more than relativity leads to relativism or dialectics to sophistics. It is a necessary consequence of the new concept of the real, which is no longer that of dogmatic materialism, and of the new concept of dialectical reason, which is no longer that of dogmatic rationalism.

Ethics again, and, more generally, our concept of relationships with others, have been profoundly affected by the same new concept. It can no longer be a matter of some vague 'tolerance', purely static, negative, and always provisional. From the dogmatic point of view, indeed, since reality is one and already complete, and truth a faithful copy of it, the man who refuses to see it can only be either sick or in bad faith: tolerance towards his hallucinations, his errors or his refusals, can lead only to an attitude that is pedagogic, therapeutic, and, quite possibly, repressive.

In contrast with this 'tolerance', dialogue, founded on a

dialectical theory of knowledge which brings out the 'active element' of knowledge in the construction of models designed to grasp the various aspects of an always plural reality, implies that we have something to learn from the other investigator, even if he is starting from other hypotheses than ours. Only experimental confrontation will enable us to integrate in a more comprehensive unitary theory, in a more complex model, what, in our initial concepts, were no more than partial and one-sided truths.

The third characteristic of this modern humanism, which derives from the first two, is the paramount part played henceforth by the notion of 'structure'.

In the tradition of classical antiquity, from Thales to Parmenides, and from Aristotle to Lucretius, the prime problem was that of Being. This problem was to persist, in the scholastics as in Descartes.

It is only with Kant and Fichte that a philosophy of *act* challenges the philosophy of *being*.

The present success of 'structuralism' may be explained both by the fact that it is a *philosophy* which corresponds to the concept of the world emerging, in the middle of the twentieth century, from the development of the whole body of natural and human sciences; and by the fact that there is derived from this concept of the world a *method* of investigation whose applications to the most diverse disciplines have proved to be extremely fruitful—as, for example, in cybernetics. Moreover, the fruitfulness of the method is even greater when structuralism and cybernetics effect their conjunction in a dialectical perspective.

The notion of 'structure' in the modern sense of the term comports a philosophy. We may call it, as a first rough approximation: a philosophy whose fundamental category is no longer *being* but *relation*. The connection between this approach and the 'operational' character of knowledge can readily be appreciated. If reality cannot be defined outside the technical or intellectual operations by which we understand it and can handle it, then the concern of knowing is no longer to arrive at the *contemplation of prime elements* or ultimate principles by which each moment takes on a *meaning* and a reality as a function of the part it plays within the whole.

From the modern, operational, concept of reason, there necessarily derives the key idea of structuralism: that of the primacy of relation towards being, and of the whole towards the parts. For it is no longer a question of getting back to prime elements in order to conceive relation only as a *rapport extrinsic* to and *subordinate* to the elements; on the contrary, we have to recognise that what we have agreed to call the element has no meaning or reality except through the knot of relationships that constitute it. In all disciplines, structuralism is taking the place of atomism.

Ferdinand de Saussure has expressed its fundamental formula in connection with linguistics: 'It is a great illusion to regard a term simply as the union of a certain sound with a certain concept. To define it so would be to isolate it from the system of which it forms a part. It would be to believe that one can begin with terms and build up the system by adding them all up, whereas, on the contrary, it is from the integral whole that we must start if we are to obtain by analysis the elements it contains' (*Cours de linguistique générale*, 4th edition, p. 157).

Starting from the study of language, de Saussure establishes two principles whose scope extends beyond linguistics and applies to all fields of culture, of science and of the arts: units can be defined only by their relationships: they are forms and not substances.

The science which has progressed most rapidly since the beginning of the twentieth century and has most contributed to transforming the traditional image of matter, is physics: and physics provides a striking illustration of this inversion of perspective. Nuclear and relativity physics no longer conceive matter as a collection of atoms, compact particles or indivisible globules, in which nothing takes place and which are linked together by external relationships—like the atoms of Lucretius or the planets of the Newtonian universe: it sees them as fields of energy in which forces and tensions that run through the whole field build up and relax at individual points, as waves rise and sink in the sea.

The triumph of this point of view sounded the death-knell of all forms of empiricism, of positivism, of scientism, with their dogmatic concept of fact as 'thing', and of 'law' as constant relationship between 'facts'.

The human sciences are receiving from the same source a valuable stimulus in the battle against the old atomism which is being fought both in sociology and psychology.

Marxism, whose founder laid down the basic principle that 'the individual is the sum total of his social relationships' (sixth thesis on Feuerbach), was able to find in this both a confirmation of one of its major theses and a most fruitful development of the notion of 'structure' which Marx used in his *Introduction to the Critique of Political Economy*, where he emphasises so forcibly the predominance of the whole over the parts and of relationships over individuals.

Structuralism makes it possible to combat both the idealist and metaphysical concept of an 'essence of man' defined without reference to social relationships and history, and the mechanistic and positivist concept of an essence of things defined once and for all without reference to scientific 'models' which enable us to grasp the real and give it meaning as a function of a whole organic system of concepts: a system which has a history and is subject, in the development of that history, to overall revisions and reorganisations which leave no principle and no element unincluded. Thus structuralism is an excellent antidote to dogmatism.

It is an antidote, too, to the positivist temptation always to explain the higher by the lower, the system by the element, neglecting what, in the whole, cannot be reduced to the parts which constitute it: and that is precisely the structure, in other words the system of relationships from which each element receives its meaning and reality.

This notion of 'structure' has been enriched by contributions from other sciences, making clear its relationship with 'Gestalt' in psychology, with the theory of 'sets' in mathematics, with the notion of the cybernetic 'model': with that of organisation, too, in biology, of 'form' in aesthetics and with the whole body of discoveries from those in chemistry to those in political economy, from physics to the fine arts.

The psychology of form has already accustomed us to not comprehending a form except in its relation to an underlying foundation, to regarding it as a whole which cannot be reduced to the sum of its parts, to conceiving the persistence of the form through the transposition of the elements which constitute it, this 'invariable' which constitutes the meaning of a passage throughout the multiplicity of its translations, or through musical transposition when the notes are changed but the same intervals are retained.

In mathematics the theory of sets defines a body of unsupported relationships, of abstract groups which can be 'realised' in 'isomorphous' concrete sets.

The cybernetic 'model' can be regarded as a conceptual or technological 'realisation' of a 'structure'.

A 'model' is always the formal representation of a body of relationships, of a structure. But the cybernetic model presents dialectical characteristics which its constructor has, consciously or unconsciously, introduced into it. It is precisely these which make it, partially, equated with the natural phenomena under investigation, and to this is due its efficiency as an instrument of research. To this again, conversely, is due the ability of the model method to assist in revealing the existence of a dialectic of nature. If dialectical models are efficient instruments of research, they to some degree justify a dialectical representation of the object under examination. The model method thus represents an experimental investigation of the dialectic of nature.

As M. Guillaumaud has shown in his *Cybernétique et matérialisme dialectique,* cybernetics, as the general theory of the properties of auto-regulating systems, by constantly operating in imitation of the living organism, offers the best road to the research of a dialectical reason.

In the first place, this is because the fundamental notion of 'feed-back' gives a concrete content to the dialectic of contradictions: an auto-regulating system is one in which every variation is the cause of its own negation. Servo-mechanism is a technical realisation of *external contradiction,* too, since this resistance to the variations entails a reaction on the whole of the system, allowing it, through constant inversion of its relationship with the environment, to function without variation.

A second characteristic of the cybernetic model's implicit dialectic is that it integrates time with logic, in the form of irreversible relationships: when an electronic machine, as for example, Dr Grey Walter's tortoise, imitates the acquisition of conditioned reflexes, stores corrections to behaviour almost as though it were being trained, it obliges us to think of it as we have to think of life itself: to think of it, that is, not in an analytical way, as made up of interchangeable elements independent of one another, but in a synthetic way, as a sum total of relationships situated in a concrete time, and hier-archically disposed in an order of increasing complexity.

Here, however, we must note the boundary which divides the most highly perfected of dialectical machines from the living being: even though the former can maintain its balance with the environment and even complexify its be-haviour by correcting it in the light of set-backs, it cannot 'adapt itself' in the sense in which a living species does so, that is, by changing its own 'structure' and so transforming itself into another type of organism with a new structure and new programmes.

Thus the theory of cybernetic models, following a road which Apostel was the first to open up, can make it possible

to give an increasingly more accurate and richer content to
the categories of dialectic: feedback providing a concrete
model of reciprocal action and of contradiction, irreversibility giving a first approximation of the process of becoming,
of physical time, structure making it possible to think of the
category of totality as a function of the new image of the
world which the sciences are giving us in this last third of
the twentieth century.

It is because of this that structuralism is not only a
philosophy, a concept of the world, but also a method.

The method which derives from this concept of the world
is in the first place a rigorous application of *reasoning by
analogy*. In the past reasoning by analogy has already lain
at the root of great discoveries, by transposing into new
fields, as working hypotheses, a knowledge which has been
gained in another science.

Structuralism, enriched by the mathematical theory of sets
and the cybernetic theory of models, makes it possible in the
first place to carry into a discipline the results obtained from
the study of isomorphous structures in another discipline:
this has been attempted, for example, by Lévi-Strauss for
systems of blood-relationships and linguistic systems. Another
outstanding example is biological and physiological investigation which is based on cybernetic models of certain structures and functions of elements in the nervous system.

By bringing out valid laws of correlation or development,
at different degrees of complexity and at all levels of the real,
from physics to sociology, from biology to aesthetics, the
methods of structuralism and cybernetics have given to the
notion of 'dialectic of nature' put forward by Engels both
its most striking confirmation and immense possibilities for
research and development.

When structuralism linked up with cybernetics, the theory
of information made it possible to enter a new stage by
giving analogy a mathematical form and providing it with
an instrument of measurement. From biology to aesthetics,

the theory of information supplies a method of calculating increasing complexity of structures. Whether we are dealing with the formation of increasingly more complex and more improbable living organisms, with ever higher values of what Brillouin calls a 'structural negative or counter-entropy' (*néguentropie*), or with the creation of new forms of art, the theory of information cannot substitute a method of calculation for a value-judgment, but it can provide value-judgments (which ultimately derive from ends postulated by man) with the objective basis of its method of calculation.

Thus the structural method not only enables us to meet new facts with hypotheses of structure suggested by other disciplines, and so to anticipate and foresee; it also invites us to understand the meaning and reality of each fact by re-setting it within a wider totality in virtue of which the fact takes on a meaning and a reality. The application of the structural method to the sociology of literature has proved fruitful, even if the first attempts are tainted by a certain mechanicism. Even more fruitful has been its application, by Pierre Francastel, to the sociology of art: Francastel, reacting against the preconception according to which a society has a structure completely determined by economics, politics, and social life, with art having nothing to do except to express or translate it, has brought out the role of art as not only an expression of values but also a participation in the creation of values. Thus he has developed a method of deciphering works of art and, through them, the society in which they are produced. This method rules out both the mechanism of Taine, which reduces aesthetics to a theory of the symbol, and the idealism of Wölfflin or Focillon, which attributes to forms an autonomous life and development. 'Wölfflin and Focillon have failed to take into consideration the notion of structure,' he writes in *La realité figurative*, p. 18. Conceiving art as one of the moments of the continued creation of man by man, the creation of new reality and new values, Francastel does not treat it only as a superstructure, as though the function of art was to reproduce and hallow a pre-existing reality (after the fashion of a crude mechanistic Marxism), but as a necessary dialectical moment of the structure of human society as it moulds its own features.

In this he has given Marxism a source of development, starting from a concept of the world and of man which corresponds to the contemporary orientation of the sciences and arts.

The prospects opened up for Marxist research by structuralism and cybernetics rule out dogmatic, mechanistic, reifying ('*chosiste*'), interpretations of materialism, and the equally dogmatic, speculative, theological interpretations of dialectic.

What has served to obscure this great truth has been, on the one hand, the over-hasty attempts, of which Norbert Wiener himself (even though he saw and pointed out the danger) very soon provided a bad example, to apply cybernetics to the handling of men in society. These attempts derived not from the principles of cybernetics but from the technocratic ideas of some of its pioneers. This confusion has now been cleared up.

The same cannot be said of structuralism, which is still regarded by many Marxists with suspicion.

This is due no doubt to the fact that there is still confusion between the essential principles of structuralism as a concept of the world and as a method, and the way in which they have been expressed by some of its best-known representatives.

For example, in Lévi-Strauss, whose scientific work is among the most fruitful of our time, the structural method is brought into operation from a starting point in personal postulates which are in no way part of this method, and which even, to my mind, contradict its spirit.

We need do no more than quote three of these.

1. The postulate according to which all structures can ultimately be reduced to mental structures: 'temporal modalities of universal laws in which the unconscious activity of the

mind consists.' This sort of transcendental structuralism, which has Kantian and, ultimately, idealist echoes, in no way derives from the principles of the method. On the contrary it appears to contradict them by according a privileged position to such structures, of which others would be no more than the expression: an attitude, rightly denounced by Francastel, which is the reciprocal of a crude mechanism and sees in cultural works no more than an epiphenomenon of infrastructures.

2. The postulate (which derives, moreover, from the first) according to which structure is not a reality but only a programme. For Lévi-Strauss, the structure is not 'the nucleus of the object' but 'the relational system latent in the object'. Here the problem seems to me to be wrongly expressed, since this opposition between the object and the relations which constitute it contradicts the very principle of structuralism, whose great merit is to have, if not abolished, at least dialecticised this opposition.

3. The postulate which opposes structure to history. Lévi-Strauss admits that there are not only synchronic but also diachronic structures. 'I do not mean to reject the notion of process,' he says, 'nor to dispute the importance of dynamic interpretations.' Nevertheless, he introduces a radical cleavage between the method of ethnology and that of history: 'ethnology is a witness alien to the group' whose structure he is studying, while 'no process exists except for a subject involved in its own historical becoming.' Temporality is always lived by a subject, and history is accordingly, on principle, tainted with subjectivity.

Without entering into an argument on the fundamentals of the problem, it seems in no way to follow from structuralism that 'laws of development' cannot be regarded as structures and that they, more than other structures, are, on principle, impatient of objective study.

To reduce history to the lived and the event-al makes it impossible any longer to understand transition from one structure to another. It would appear that Lévi-Strauss's exclusivism is due to chance circumstances: as an ethnologist, his studies have been confined exclusively to societies that are no longer evolving, societies that have become stabilised in the mere reproduction of one and the same cycle. Thus there was no serious methodological disadvantage in studying only their 'synchronic' structures. But why should not the notion of structure, valid for the anatomy of societies, be applied to their physiology? How can one define the structure of an organ if one leaves out of account its function? And how can one fully study its function and structure without studying its history? Biological evolution offers us models of 'laws of development'; why, when we come to look at specifically human history, should their study suddenly become subjective, while it is admitted as a postulate that one can study objectively the synchronic structures of a society even though the observer's judgments of value and prejudices may also be a confusing influence in that study? For example, when Lévi-Strauss continually finds the same mental structures at work 'in primitive thought' or in the thought with which we are familiar, surely his observation is distorted by a Kantian *a priorism* which derives from the culture proper to his own society?

If we dismiss these contingent postulates, structuralism can, like cybernetics, be one of the ways of comprehending the world and of conceiving man and his action, which corresponds the best to the spirit of our time, to the development of a new humanism: this will be precisely the humanism of which Marx was the pioneer, integrating all that was won by Graeco-Roman humanism and Judaeo-Christian humanism, and going beyond both in a new synthesis of nature and man, of the external world and subjectivity, of necessary law and liberty.

CHAPTER THREE

Marxism and Ethics

*

To rediscover the fundamental inspiration of Marxism, as defined by Marx in his *Contribution to the Critique of Hegel's Philosophy of Right* ('to be radical is to grasp things by the root. But for man the root is man himself', in *Early Writings*, p. 52), is never to forget that Marxism is not a pre-critical, dogmatic, philosophy.

The key idea of all critical (non-dogmatic) philosophy is that human experience forms a whole. The specific characteristic of dogmatism, on the contrary, is the detaching of one aspect of the total experience and the claim to explain the whole in terms of one of its parts. For example, an idealist metaphysics attributes a privileged value to ideas, and endeavours to reconstruct the world as a tissue of intelligible relationships; correspondingly, a metaphysical and mechanistic materialism seeks to explain the world from the properties of matter as conceived by science at some particular historical stage of its development.

The critical attitude starts by rejecting these arbitrary options. The principle that governs its method is that every moment of total experience forms one with all others and forms one with a history. We cannot overstep our own shadow: we can never define once and for all either concept or matter; and every philosophy is dogmatic which claims to establish itself in the concept, like Plato or even Spinoza, or to establish itself in matter, like d'Holbach or the Stalinist interpretation of Marxism.

If we rigorously follow up the consequences of this rejection of dogmatism in every field, we are obliged to re-think, in the spirit of our time, the significance of Marxism in the theory of knowledge as in moral science, too, or in aesthetics.

Just as Bachelard established the necessity for a 'non-Cartesian epistemology', just as Bertold Brecht called his aesthetics 'non-Aristotelian', just as the writings of Simondon study the significance of 'dialectical machines' from the point of view of what I might call a 'non-Laplacian technology', so it becomes necessary to conceive a 'non-Platonist' ethic: one, in other words, which does not start from the concept, traditional in the West since Hellenism, that man's behaviour is 'right' when it conforms to a rule, an ideal, or a pre-existing model.

Thus the moral problem, like the problem of knowledge, is reversed. When we ask ourselves what we must do if we are to act rightly, we are not seeking to conform to a pre-existing law or to a being that is already 'given': we are asking ourselves what must be brought into existence which is not yet existing.

This ethic, which is history in process of being made, a specifically human history and one whose scenario has not been written by any god or any fate, nor by any abstract dialect (whether it be the absolute mind of Hegel or the 'inevitable progress' of the eighteenth-century materialists)— this ethic is the continued creation of man by man.

At no moment is this creation arbitrary, and at no moment is it determined. Man is totally responsible for becoming not what he is but what he is not yet and what is nowhere set down; and at the same time he is obliged to be conscious of the historical conditions created by man's earlier creations, which obey necessary laws, to neglect or make light of which leads to fortuity and impotence.

Marx's essential discovery in moral science lies in this, that, first by his historical and militant rather than Hegelian and Feuerbachian concept of alienation, and later by his demonstration in *Capital*, he 'liquidated' into human acts what had been crystallised in things and historical situations, thus showing man that it was possible for him to revindicate his claim to control his own destiny.

To show, as Marx did, how man's act in continuing in history his own creation is at the same time and indivisibly necessary and free, was to lay the theoretical foundation of all revolutionary action, and the theoretical foundation, too, of all moral science, sacrificing neither objective necessity to personal responsibility nor the element of subjectivity to the consciousness of inflexible laws of development.

In this Marxist attitude to man and his history, the moral problem cannot be shelved: it cannot be replaced by the scientific and technical problem of truth, of the search for and discovery of a *true* order of things and of nature which would give to moral conduct a foundation external to man.

The study of laws of social development, the possibility even of plotting, at least in its essentials, the trajectory of a more or less probable immediate or distant future, does not at any time excuse us from making ourselves conscious of our own responsibility as *subjects* who act and create our own history, and not as *objects* of a history in a concept that would reduce us to being no more than the resultant or sum of the conditions of our existence.

The moral problem is not a simple problem; neither simple as the blind acceptance of rules of conduct given to us ready-made from outside, nor as the affirmation of a radical freedom to determine ourselves, and by ourselves alone, our values and ends.

In a man's life, the moral problem is made up of contradictions that are lived and continually reborn, between the demands of the discipline that is indispensable to the effectiveness of our struggle, and the sense of personal responsibility of each one of us in both the working out and the application of the very laws which govern our fighting.

If a Marxist is to answer the question of the relationship

between moral behaviour and society, he has to solve three problems:

(a) He must finally and permanently break with dogmatism by emphasising that Marxism is not a pre-critical philosophy, and that one cannot think as a Marxist if one thinks as though Kant and Fichte had never existed. This means that we must not reduce the legacy of classical German philosophy in Marxism to Hegel and Feuerbach; we must reappraise the legacy of Kant and Fichte by setting it once again firmly on its feet, that is to say by showing that a dialectical materialist concept of practice enables us to develop a critical philosophy without succumbing to the idealist illusion that our activity engenders the reality on which it is exerted.

(b) He must work out more profoundly the Marxist theory of subjectivity by recognising that existentialism has raised a real problem, even if we cannot accept either the way in which it expresses the problem or the answer it provides; remembering, too, that the study of the problem of subjectivity is not necessarily associated with a subjectivist and individualist conception.

(c) He must work out a Marxist theory of dialectical transition which enables us to explore all the dimensions of man, including those of interiority and of values, without falling into alienated theological concepts, which make transcendence an attribute not of man but of God.

It goes without saying that in speaking of transcendence there is no question of retaining either the word or the idea in the traditional sense, which is closely linked to the 'supernatural'; beneath the alienations and mystifications which have attributed to gods the power which man possesses of going beyond the situation imposed on him by nature or society, we have to rediscover this constant fundamental experience: that man cannot be reduced to the sum total of the conditions which have produced him; as man, he exists only by going beyond them.

These few remarks on moral science are, accordingly, inspired by the threefold concern to discover how Marxism can develop:

a critical philosophy which is not idealist
a theory of subjectivity which is not subjective
a theory of dialectical transition which is not alienated.

*

Ethics appears in the first place as a body of laws regulating our conduct. Every man has a moral system which has come to him from outside, through education, in other words in virtue of the fact that the individual belongs to a society, to an historical and social community.

This is our experience as children, for whom what is forbidden and what is allowed are imposed from outside, as a fact. Initially, right and wrong have the same at once conventional and inexorable character as the green and the red light.

The whole body of these rules constitutes a sort of scenario in which a precise 'job' is laid down for us: all we have to do is to put on the costume and act the part. Thus, from my very infancy, I belong to a religion, a country, a class, a family, a tradition and so on, of which the ends and the means of attaining them appear to me as intangible 'values'; the problem of their basis does not arise, any more, indeed, than that of transgression.

How is the transition to be effected from this 'constituted' morality to 'constituent' morality? From pure and simple acceptance of social constraint to the development of consciousness of personal responsibility?

The foundation of morality does not, initially, appear as a problem.

It is imposed in the form of myth, by a didactic story or as something revealed by a transcendent intervention, from the code of Hammurabi to the Mosaic Decalogue.

In a reflective form, it can still not be a problem, but rather a justification, as is shown by the purely sociological theories whose general characteristic is to reduce value to truth, and to claim to give, in the form of an objective description of a human social nature, both an explanation and a justification of obligation or contract.

This ideology of justification clothes itself in the trappings of 'reason', each social class, in the course of history, having qualified as 'rational' what is consonant with its own class interests. From Menenius Agrippa's fable of the belly and the limbs to Herbert Spencer's organological theories, and from Plato's personification of 'Laws' to Hegel's *Philosophy of Right*, these ideologies of justification have taken over from myth and revelation.

How, then, are we to present the problem of the underlying basis, the problem of the value of values? How can we move from the mythical or revealed plane of the given, and the ideological plane of justification, to the tragic plane of questioning and responsibility?

By starting from the lived experience of contradiction.

Contradiction can be lived in many ways at a rupture-point in history, either because there has been external conflict between different communities and a collision with the gods of other cities has opposed a fact to a fact, a moral system to another moral system, or because the internal development of a society has opened up for its members new prospects and possibilities that make the old norms intolerable and thereby, too, create the conditions for a rebellion or a secession. Historical crisis and personal drama are then closely interwoven. This is the Promethean moment of ethics: the moment to which Antigone gave the tragic features of the revolt of conscience against the old law, the Socratic moment of doubt and challenge of which Descartes, at the threshold of the modern age, provided the most inflexible example.

Each of our experiences brings us back to this. The contradiction that is most generally lived, for example between the Kantian demand never to consider the individual as a means but always as an end, and the social reality of the capitalist régime which makes the wage-earning worker a means for the production of surplus value, provides a striking picture of the daily radical divorce of an avowed moral ideal and an actual social reality.

We have only to take another look at Max Weber's demonstration in his *The Protestant Ethic and the Spirit of Capitalism* to see how each economic and social formation distils its own morality as an ideology of justification—as Engels showed when, in his *Anti-Dühring*, he analysed, inside capitalism, the survival of a feudal morality, the domination of a bourgeois morality and the coming into being of a proletarian morality.

Thus we find that, by personal experience of lived contradiction and by the contradictory development of societies, we are brought back to the initial antinomy of constituted morality and constituent morality, and are again faced by the need to establish a dialectical relationship, that is to say a relationship simultaneously of exclusion and of mutual involvement, between these two poles. If we reduce morality to a system of social rules, we shall inevitably fall into dogmatism; and if we emphasise the conscious basis exclusively, we shall inevitably fall into formalism, and ultimately into a morality of intention.

To one who confines himself solely to the point of view of the social rule, the individual who challenges the rule by questioning himself about the value of these values, seems to be already on the road to *betrayal*.

To one who confines himself to the point of view of the individual conscience, and never succeeds in emerging from his ˜cogito´, the rule itself already appears as an *alienation*.

This is the antinomy we have to overcome.

The difficulty appears as soon as a consciously critical philosophy is built up. Kant found that he had to direct the first preface to his *Critique of Pure Reason* against *dogmatism* and to emphasise in his second the battle against *scepticism*.

The problem of the transition from freedom to law, that is, the problem of the dialectical unity of the form and content of morality, was raised for the first time in its full force by Fichte in his *Sittenlehre*. In this *System of moral science* the first chapter is directed against dogmatism. Its aim is to lay down the first principle: the freedom of the ego, ruling out all transcendence, both transcendence from above—that of God and his revealed commandments—and transcendence from below, that of the thing as datum. The second chapter, by contrast, is directed against formalism, and aims at providing morality with a concrete content.

Fichte thus offers us an exemplary model of the effort to keep hold of both ends of the chain, ethics and society.

The compound was so unstable that its unity was soon broken:

with Hegel there is already a return to dogmatism, which makes subjectivity a moment of objective morality, but one that is so completely and definitively left behind that the individual subject has no existence or value except as a function of the rational and social totality.

with Stirner and also, from a very different point of view, with Kierkegaard, it is the totality, the social totality for the former and the rational totality for the latter, which is abandoned: in the case of Stirner, in favour of the exclusive affirmation of the 'Unique', of the individual; in the case of Kierkegaard, in virtue of the tragic colloquy of subjectivity and transcendence, which involves, if Christ is not to be crucified on the cross of concept, the abandonment of the rational, the historical, and the social.

The present issue between Marxism and existentialism can be classified in this historical perspective. Does not Sartre to some extent renew, in relation to Marxism or to the idea he has formed of it, the protest made by Kierkegaard against Hegel? And cannot we Marxists, inspired by Fichte's efforts to keep hold of both ends of the chain, interiorise and integrate Sartre's demand and so make of it an element of our own thought?

A Marxism which never forgets Kant or Fichte, a Marxism,

that is, which never forgets Marx or Lenin, is a critical and non-dogmatic philosophy in this sense, first of all, that it makes *practice* the source and the criterion of every truth and every value.

This entails the consequence that *experience* must not be conceived, as it is by empiricists, as an immediate contact with being and a passive reflection of a reality which is given ready-made once and for all; it rules out, too, the dogmatic claim to entrench oneself in being and to be able to say once and for all what it is. Experience is of the order of a *question*, and, in consequence, the *answer* is necessarily a function of the *question*, in other words, a function of the state of the sciences at the time the question is asked. This emphasises the historical and always historically relative character of knowledge, and makes Marxism a more consistent critical philosophy than Kant's, whose immutable table of 'categories' constitutes a hang-over from dogmatism.

In other words, Marxism *is not a philosophy of being*, that is, a philosophy like that of the scholastic theologians or the mechanist materialists, in which consciousness is at the most an image, and always (in Plato no less than in Epicurus) an impoverished image, of the reality which produces it. Such a philosophy, by identifying consciousness and knowledge, leads to the suppression of subjectivity, retaining only what is impersonal and external to consciousness; and by conceiving truth, as St Thomas Aquinas did, for example, as identity with being, it leads to the suppression of all real becoming, all authentic historicity.

Marxism *is a philosophy of act*, that is, one which makes of consciousness and the human practice which engenders it and constantly enriches it a true reality, rooted in earlier activity and in the real, and reflecting them, but constantly going beyond the given and continually adding to reality by a creative act, which is not yet given at the level of pre-human nature and the success of which nothing can guarantee in advance.

84

From this it follows that for us Marxists morality is not sanctioned by nature but created by history.

How are we to relate the Marxist concept of subjectivity to existentialism?

In the first place we may say that the merit of existentialism is that, since Kierkegaard, it has shown that dogmatic rationalism, even in its richest, Hegelian, form, has, in reducing consciousness to knowledge, robbed itself of a dimension, the dimension of subjectivity. Now reason, in eliminating the *false*, does not eliminate the *fault*.

Subjectivity is in the first place the affirmation of the impossibility for consciousness of being equated with itself. Even if consciousness can at times be equated with *being*, can make it transparent to itself, it cannot be equated with its own *act* by which it necessarily transcends and creates itself.

Subjectivity, therefore, is of the order not of *being* but of *act*.

Hence the emphasis laid by existentialism on the negative experiences of error, of anguish, of check.

Hence, too, the refusal to dissociate *ideas* from the progress of existence, the justified concern to link thought to a creation of being, in the consciousness that to exist is an act, a creation.

There could be no room for the theory of subjectivity in:

a metaphysical rationalism such as that of Plato, of Spinoza, of d'Holbach or of Hegel, which by giving a privileged position to the notion of truth (conceived as identity of thought and being) could never grasp what is impersonal in us.

but there is ample room for it in a critical rationalism such as that of Kant, or Fichte, or of Marx, which is not content to discover the idea immanent in being and reduce it to that, but makes use of the idea in order to transform existence.

Existentialism is not a philosophy but an attitude towards philosophy, one that consists in regarding philosophy not as a picture of life but as a leavening of life.

If that were the case it would be true to say that Marxism

can and must be approached from an existential point of view.

Existentialism raises a real problem, even if, let me repeat, a Marxist cannot accept either the way in which it presents the problem or the solution it offers.

Marxism makes it possible to present the problem more correctly and to provide an answer to it.

To demonstrate that this is so, we must recall the situation in which existentialism was born and developed.

Historically, as Guéroult showed at the Philosophical Congress in Mexico, the original source of existentialism is to be found in Fichte.

Fichte's work was produced at a rupture-point in history. Guéroult has very rightly noted that Fichte is the only philosopher by whom the French Revolution was seen as a fact and not an idea.

Fichte's work, then, lies at a moment in history in which there is a collapse of traditional, that is, of feudal, values; at a moment when there arises the problem of the illogicality of the existing order, of the failure of faith, of conflicts between conscience and obedience. This situation explains the exaltation of the importance of the individual, of his radical autonomy, of the supreme value accorded to freedom as the mother of all values, and to responsibility.

Fichte's first thesis was thus to be the affirmation of the ego, postulating itself by itself. For the first time in the history of philosophy the primacy of essence over existence was overthrown. Man is not the expression of an essence defined *a priori*. He is nothing other than what his own free activity makes him; every man makes himself what he is. In the phrase of the Fichtean Lequier, re-adopted by Sartre, 'To make and in making to make oneself, and to be nothing other than what one makes.' 'Man is nothing but what he makes of himself.' That is what Sartre calls 'the first principle of existentialism' (*Existentialism and Humanism*, trans. Philip Mairet, London, 1948, p. 28).

86

The second thesis is that the self can be seen in fixed conceptual terms, as showing forth the ambiguity of subject and object, of constituent and constituted, of facticity[1] and freedom.

The third thesis is that the absolute ego is absolute freedom; but the constraint inherent in its make-up involves, besides the existence of choice, the obligation to choose. Fichte's fourth thesis, from which existentialism derives, is that the ego is project: it continually leaps ahead of itself, urged on by the unrealisable desire to win or create what it lacks, in other words always to be both in-self (*an sich*) and for-self (*für sich*).

In short, we find in Fichte all the key themes of existential philosophy, but within a rationalist philosophy.

Fichte can help us to keep hold of both ends of the chain. It is on the meeting ground of Fichte's philosophy that dialogue on moral science can be most fruitful: if, that is, Marxists learn again to integrate the theory of subjectivity to be found in Fichte's existential thought, and if contemporary existentialists do not mutilate Fichtean existentialism by depriving it of two fundamental dimensions: the rational dimension and the social dimension.

This mutilation, it is true, goes back a long time. The rational dimension was already abandoned by the irrationalism of Kierkegaard, and the social dimension by the individualism of Stirner. Thus the existential attitude has suffered from the parasitic activities of irrationalism, subjectivism, and formalism.

Today we have to try to win back what has been lost.

Existentialism has played an important part in the demystification of morality, as has been shown by Wanda Ban-

---

[1] 'The for-itself's necessary connection with the in-itself, hence with the world and its own past. It is what allows us to say that the for-itself *is* or *exists*. The facticity of freedom is the fact that freedom is not able "not to be free" ' (*Being and Nothingness*, trans. Hazel E. Barnes, London, 1966: from the 'Key to special terminology', p. 631).

87

nour in the emphasis she has given to a number of themes in moral criticism. Their formulation can be found again in Simone de Beauvoir's 'morality of ambiguity'.

'The moral world is not a given world.'

'There are no unconditioned ends outside of ourselves.'

'Freedom is the source from which arise all significance and all value.'

In his *Being and Nothingness* (p. 722) Sartre was already writing, 'The moral agent is the being through whom values exist.'

'. . . it is then that his freedom will become conscious of itself and will reveal itself in anguish as the unique source of value' (p. 627).

'There is *sérieux*[1] [I would prefer *alienation*, but I am not going to quibble over words. R.G.] as soon as freedom resigns in favour of ends which are chained to be absolute. The "serious" man questions nothing.'

'The specific characteristic of the "serious man" is that he regards values as things which are ready made.' This is the position of the child, who from the very beginning finds himself within a constituted morality.

'To exist is to make oneself'; it is in some way the triumph of freedom over facticity.

All these critical and Fichtean themes are common to both of us. No one can think and act in my place, no one can dispense me from the meaningfulness of my acts and from my responsible decision. No God, and no authority can make decisions for me.

It is at that point that our paths begin to diverge.

In this existentialist concept there seem to me to be two fundamental shortcomings:

1. This concept of freedom is non-temporal and extra-

---

[1] 'The "spirit of seriousness" (*l'esprit de sérieux*) views man as an object and subordinates him to the world. It thinks of values as having an absolute existence independent of human reality' (*Being and Nothingness*, 'Key to special terminology', p. 634).

historical: to put it briefly, it is metaphysical and speculative. It can be formulated at any moment you please in history; it affirms, legitimately, my right to secede, my duty to question. But if the source of values is extra-historical, it can never validate an historical, that is a concrete, end.

2. It leads, accordingly, to a moral formalism; it calls us to freedom, to responsibility, to courage, to mastery of self —which is excellent—but it does not tell us towards what end we are to use them.

It is perfectly legitimate to distinguish ends and values.

Here, however, they are opposed to one another, they are isolated from one another: I confront each situation as a pretext for the exercise of my freedom—so much so that formalism condemns us to oscillate between the desert of withdrawal and the intoxication of adventure. 'They discover at the same time,' writes Sartre (*Being and Nothingness*), 'that all human activities are equivalent . . . and that all are on principle doomed to failure. Thus it amounts to the same thing whether one is a solitary drunkard or a leader of nations. If one of these activities takes precedence over the other, this will not be because of its real goal, but because of the degree of consciousness it possesses of its ideal goal' (p. 627).

Sartre often says that his thought has developed since *Being and Nothingness* and that it is wrong to base criticism of his present concepts upon that book. In that case, however, Sartre should tell us exactly which are the theses in *Being and Nothingness* which he has now abandoned. Now, while it is obvious that for the last twenty-five years he has realised the shortcomings of a chapter such as that which he devoted to 'being for others' (*Being and Nothingness*, pp. 221ff), in which he completely neglected the notion of class, it seems no less obvious that the *Critique de la Raison dialectique* does not imply the abandonment of any of the fundamental theses of *Being and Nothingness*; and that applies particularly to those which, with his concept of liberty, provided a basis for that despairing individualism which has never allowed him to find a point at which he can insert himself in concrete history.

This freedom, emancipated from all terrestrial gravity, this angelism, involves the temptation of purity and the temptation of adventure.

This formalism develops into the most typical formulas of the moralities of intention. Since Simone de Beauvoir attempted to apply these principles to moral problems, it is from her that I shall borrow an illustration of my theme. She writes, for example, 'Do what you must, whatever happens.' 'That is,' she adds, 'the result is not external to the good will which is realised in aiming at it.'

What we have, then, is an abstract, formal, metaphysical freedom: 'We are free here and now and absolutely, if we choose to will our existence in its finiteness which opens out on to the infinite' (*Morale de l'ambiguïté*, p. 229).

The practical consequences of such a concept are formidable. Here is an example: 'The Resistance laid no claim to a positive effectiveness: it was negation, revolt, martyrdom. In the moment of refusal the antinomy of action is removed, the end and the means come together; freedom postulates itself immediately as its own end and is realised in postulating itself' (pp. 190 and 217).

Thus, it was not, according to Simone de Beauvoir, a matter of destroying the German armed forces but only of digging a moral ditch between occupiers and occupied which would make collaboration impossible.

Here is yet another example (p. 172): 'Man has always been at war and always will be.'

In such a point of view there is a radical opposition between ethics and politics. We are a long way here from the vitalising teaching of the French eighteenth-century materialists: from that of Helvetius, for example, who wrote that 'ethics would be a frivolous science if it were not identified with politics and legislation.' In Simone de Beauvoir we find such expressions as this: 'The freedom of a single man should count for more than a crop of cotton or rubber.' That represents a position of strict individualism, for the crop can mean life or death for everyone. In Cuba, for example, the sugar crop is an event upon which the life of a whole people depends, and to sabotage it calls for summary justice and execution.

In consequence, existentialism does not provide a solution to our problem. With existentialism we let go of one end of the chain. A right and proper concern to emphasise the constituent had made us lose sight of the constituted.

There can be no doubt that such a concept tends to sharpen our sense of responsibility; but at the same time it makes us forget that I am not responsible only to myself but also to a society, a class, a nation.

Where, then, does the basic mistake lie?

To provide morality with a basis, one must show that freedom cannot be divorced from the content of action: and Sartre's initial individualism bars him from the passage from one to the other.

In *Being or Nothingness*, after having found freedom in a rigorously solitary *cogito*, Sartre reduces all human relationships to 'looking'. No doubt, in his idiom, the 'look' has a symbolic value; it expresses a relationship between the self and the other, but the specific characteristic of this relationship, of this look, is that it transforms every subject into object.

The look of the other fixes me as an object: 'As the other rises up it confers on the *for-self* a being *in-self* in the midst of the world, as a thing among things. This petrification by the look of the other is the underlying significance of the myth of Medusa' (p. 502).

When we turn from *Being and Nothingness* to the *Critique de la Raison dialectique*, we find no fundamental change.

Social relationships are hardly more than a multiplication of personal relationships: that, it would seem, is the fundamental postulate of the *Critique de la Raison dialectique*. We build up the social by starting from the individual. Sartre weaves the web of history from individual projects which mutually reify one another.

Now, it is not possible to base history on a dialectical development of the relationship between Robinson Crusoe and Man Friday.

That, nevertheless, is Sartre's fundamental postulate: he writes, in his *Critique de la Raison dialectique*, 'The only concrete foundation of historical dialectic is the dialectical structure of individual action.'

'The whole of dialectic rests on individual praxis' (p. 163). Sartre rightly calls his concept 'a dialectical nominalism' (p. 32).

What he is trying to do is in some way to construct a society from metaphysically defined individuals, to construct history from the non-temporal, an historical materialism without matter.

It is true that the problem of the transition from the individual to society has been haunting the thought of Sartre for the last twenty-five years. As early as the Liberation of France, in *L'existentialisme est-il un humanisme?*, Sartre was trying to link freedom to a content of action. He wrote, 'In willing freedom, we discover that it depends entirely upon the freedom of others, and that the freedom of others depends upon our own . . . as soon as there is commitment, I am obliged to will the freedom of others at the same time as mine. I cannot make my freedom my aim unless I make that of others equally my aim' (*Existentialism and Humanism*, pp. 51-2).

In her *Morale de l'ambiguïté* Simone de Beauvoir was later to say, 'The existence of others as freedom . . . is the condition of my own freedom' (p. 131).

'The freedom (of the individual) can be achieved only through the freedom of others' (p. 225).

All this is unobjectionable, but it represents an inconsistency in relation to the initial postulates of existentialism.

The Kantian transition from my freedom to the freedom

of others was based on a rationalist postulate: the transcendent 'I' is prior, or rather alien, to the plurality of subjects. The problem of the transition to others does not arise if we start from the transcendental 'I'; it is impossible if we start from the existential 'I'.

That is why, in *Being and Nothingness*, Sartre rules out the possibility of this passage (as, moreover, he did in his 1939 article). 'Even if I should want to act according to the precepts of Kantian morality and take the Other's freedom as an unconditioned end, I would not be able to possess the Other as object' (p. 408).

'Respect for the Other's freedom', adds Sartre, 'is an empty word; even if we could assume the project of respecting this freedom, each attitude which we adopted with respect to the Other would be a violation of that freedom which we claimed to respect . . . to realise tolerance with respect to the Other is to cause the Other to be thrown forcibly into a tolerant world. It is to remove from him on principle those free possibilities of courageous resistance, of perseverance, of self-assertion, which he would have had the opportunity to develop in a world of intolerance' (p. 409).

In *Morale de l'ambiguïté* Simone de Beauvoir endeavours to bridge the same gulf between freedom and concrete ends by passing from my own freedom to that of others. The attempt, however, is doomed to failure even before it is made, since if I start from the individualist existential 'I', I am condemning myself to insularity and solipsism.

From the point of view of *Being and Nothingness* there is absolutely no justification for saying, 'While it is true that every project emanates from a subjectivity, it is also true that this subjective movement in itself postulates a going beyond subjectivity' (p. 103).

Or again, it is impossible to say that the self-others relationship is as indissoluble as the subject-object relationship.

There is one form of the transition which is not Kant's, which is not a transition by rationality. In Fichte the transition from self to others is effected not through the mediation of the rational, but from an existential self that is *already* inhabited by others.

The rigour of Fichte's thought enabled him to effect this transition.

He shows that the existence of others is the condition of consciousness in itself. The presence of others *is prior to the cogito*, since the ego cannot postulate itself except as limited, and 'a free activity cannot be limited by a thing but only by a free activity.'

From this it follows that my autonomy has as the condition of its freedom the freedom of the other, and, in consequence, that I cannot envisage destroying the condition of my own autonomy, that is, the freedom of the other.

This deduction of Fichte's is possible only because the starting point has not been an insular, solipsist, cogito. Fichte asserts that 'the *first* condition, which might be called the root of my individuality, is not determined through my freedom, but through my connection with another rational being' (*The Science of Ethics*, trans. A. E. Kroeger, London, 1897, p. 234).

In Fichte the pure *I* is opposed to the empirical *I* in the same way as the *we* is opposed to the *I*. This has been forcibly recalled by Gurvitch in his *Dialectique et Société*, in which he returns to the theses he had already elaborated on the moral science of Fichte. 'Our science of morals,' says Fichte, 'is therefore very important for our whole system, since in it is shown up how the empirical Ego arises out of the purely genetical Ego, and how the pure Ego is altogether externalized from the individual person. From the present point of view, the representation of the pure Ego is the totality of rational beings, or the communion of saints' (*op. cit.*, p. 270).

From this Fichte draws a conclusion of capital importance which will rule out for ever the opposition between ethics and politics. 'To each rational being, all others outside him are end; but no one is his own end. The point of view from which all individuals, without exception, are final ends, lies beyond all individual consciousness, and is the point of view from which the consciousness of all rational beings is united, an object, into One; hence the point of view of God. For God, each rational being is absolute and final end . . . he is end as a *means* to realise reason' (*Ibid*, pp. 270-1).

It was thus, and only thus, that Fichte was able to construct a theory of subjectivity which is neither subjectivist nor individualist. Thereby, too, he was able to pass from constituent morality to a constituted morality, to link together personal responsibility and the social rules of concrete morality, to bring together ethics and politics, and to respect the autonomy of moral consciousness without lapsing into formalism.

Using another road, Marxism makes this transition possible. It is noteworthy that the Marxist classics do not confuse the role of subjectivity and that of the individual. Without going as far back as Marx's criticism of Stirner, which represented the first polemic of Marxism and its first confrontation with a form of existentialism, we can give three examples of this presence of others in subjectivity:

1. In history (and in politics, which is history being made), when Lenin speaks of the *subjective factor*, he in no way limits this to the individual factor. He is concerned with classes and their action.

2. In the sciences: when contemporary physics shows us that the answers given by experiment are a function of the questions asked, these questions are not those asked by any unspecified individual, but those of a culture, of the 'physicist-city' of which Bachelard spoke. The physicist who asks the question is not only an individual: in virtue of this culture the whole of past mankind dwells in him, and in virtue of this city, the whole of present mankind dwells in him too.

3. In art: 'To paint well,' wrote Cézanne, 'is in spite of oneself to express all that is most advanced in one's time . . . a painter who knows his grammar, cannot but express on his

95

canvas what the best informed brain of his time has conceived or is conceiving . . . Giotto echoes Dante . . . Poussin echoes Descartes.' Historically, moreover, the individual never becomes conscious of himself except within a culture, that is, a community.

How can Marxism effect this transition from freedom to the content of action, the transition which is the necessary condition for laying the foundation of moral science and for the disalienation of the world?

The crucial problem is the problem of the starting point.

The Marxist cogito is not the cogito of Descartes nor that of Sartre.

It reinstates the cogito of Fichte, moving from speculation to history, from idealism to materialism.

1. *The primary experience is not that of solitude.*

The 'we' comes first in relation to the 'I'.

Man becomes conscious of himself only in his relationships with others. Reflection, that is, the relation of self to self, is possible only as exteriorisation of the relationship with others. The consciousness which addresses itself in assuming the form of an 'I', takes on the function which was fulfilled by the other consciousness.

Subjectivity is born of communication.

From the very beginning I grasp myself as an individual resting on a foundation of community.

At no moment is my project an individual project (otherwise I find myself imprisoned in solipsism).

In the first place, this is because this becoming conscious of self—this splitting, that is—is an interiorisation of a dialogue, and presupposes a *language*.

Secondly, because this language is the vehicle of a knowledge, itself implied in work, which is always a *social* work.

As early as the first reflection, as early as the first project, the whole of past and present mankind has been dwelling in me.

'The individual,' said Marx, 'is the sum total of his social relationships.' Saint-Exupéry (*Pilote de Guerre*, p. 347) was to find the same thing: 'Man is no more than a knot of relationships; only relationships count for man.'

Consciousness of self, with the split it involves, is already an interiorised dialogue: it entails, within my self, a tension between me and the other.

Kant's mistake (already corrected by Fichte) lay in having made of duty, of 'duty-to-be', a privileged experience.

'Duty-to-be' is implicit in all the moments of existence, and not simply in the feeling of duty.

The act by which I become conscious of what I am, is possible only in as much as it entails and produces a being who is already no longer what I am now: reflection holds within itself a genesis.

In the 'I am' there is infinitely more than the 'I am', since the act of affirmation transcends the content of this affirmation.

Such is the antinomy of transcendence.

Reflection and act already entail transcendence, internal duality, dialectic.

From this derives a consequence of capital importance: to be conscious is at every moment to stand at a distance from one's being, in order not only to know it but to transform it. There is thus a transcendence of mankind in relation to itself.

2. *The possible and the project.*

I am conscious of this *I* only through the presence of others in me.

This presence shows itself in the language in which I speak to myself and in the work in which I go beyond myself. Work, as the going beyond being, is the first moral category.

These are two functions of *the other*, which are both functions of transcendence.

This going beyond is the critical form of transcendence, it is the specifically human dimension, which allows us to emerge from animality, to break the circle of species and instinct, to pass from biological evolution to specifically human history. It was with this in mind that Marx said that it is with work that man is born. Now, what distinguishes man's work from animal activity (that of the beaver, the ant, the bee) is the anticipation of the act, which makes of this project the law of its action. It is this possible, this project, which enables man to move towards the future along an original road that the animal was incapable of knowing, the road that entails freedom and choice.

3. *Choice and freedom*

Man does not make a choice between *given* terms but between *possibles* (projects). Freedom is born with this possibility of projecting a number of possible acts. In action we confront the future with our possibles, just as in knowledge we confront reality with our hypotheses.

The future enters into consciousness only through the latter's projects (its possibles), just as nature enters into the consciousness of the scientist only through the question (the hypothesis) he has already formulated.

The project is the form by the act before we have accomplished it.

It is only for a free being (that is, a being who forms projects, projecting possibles ahead of himself), that a *fact* can appear upon a substratum of possibilities and have a *value*.

Value, like truth, is born of this split, in other words it is born in practice. It is born in the unity of a possible by which our freedom is expressed, of a project in which our knowledge is deployed, of a need which is the driving force of our action.

4. *Need and valorisation.*

In other words, man creates his values simultaneously with his needs, and his needs simultaneously with his possibles (as he transforms nature).

That is why when Poincaré said that science speaks in the indicative and ethics in the imperative, the opposition was based on a truncated view of man's relationship to the world, which makes of knowledge a radically independent moment.

Knowledge is the development of the activity of work.

The object is not simply the system of means; it is what meets the needs, what is adapted to human nature, not in the anthropological sense, but to human nature such as history has made it at one moment of its history, or rather such as it has made its own history.

This comprehension of social necessity is the only concrete basis of the project which reaches out to an emancipation, a true freedom.

Need is not only individual but also social. It takes the form of historical necessity, of revolt, of demand. Through it is effected the transition from alienation to revolution.

5. *Alienation.*

I do not propose to enlarge here either on the nature of alienation or on its genesis, which I have dealt with elsewhere, but to look at its relationship with the four propositions put forward above.

From the point of view of the 'we', alienation is the splitting of the 'we', its mutilation; alienation is what stands in the way of world-wide participation in human culture.

From the point of view of possibles and projects, alienation is man robbed of his specifically human dimension: the determination of possibles and projects (economic, political, cultural, etc.). This determination becomes a class privilege: the ruling class (the class which owns the means of production and the State) makes of man a means, an object.

From the point of view of choice, the ruling class arrogates to itself, in addition to the privilege of culture, a monopoly of decision and command.

Finally, from the point of view of needs, and the means of

99

satisfying them, Marx showed in *Capital* that distribution is determined by production-relationships. Values are thereby similarly determined.

In these conditions the proletarian revolution, from the middle of the nineteenth century, became a fundamental moral value and an end that is valid not as a final end or ultimate value, but as a necessary means for the emancipation and full development of man.

If we ask why this was so, the answer is that during that period there was in it a coincidence of a *possible*, a *project*, and a *need*.

Revolution is the birth of a possible, a project, and a need, and hence of a value.

(a) Birth of a possible. Scientific socialism became possible towards the second half of the nineteenth century because at that time, with the triumph of capitalism, alienation acquired a true universality.

It was then that society, as a working organism, could be comprehended as a totality.

This discovery, which was taken up again by Marx, was the work of Adam Smith and Ricardo.

And from this possible a project could be born.

(b) Birth of a project. In a society which made work its mode of existence and through work acquired its organic unity or totality, awareness of this implicit, potential, totality and action to realise it in act were one and the same thing.

Lévi-Strauss's structuralism has made us familiar with such a concept of totality, in which the rational and the operational are one and the same thing.

Now, if we look at Marx's *Capital* as a structural study of the infrastructures of capitalist society; if we see in it a 'model', in the sense in which cyberneticians use the word, of a society on a larger scale, which can function either with private ownership of the means of production and the contradictions which that involves, or in accordance with the principles of socialism, which alone can translate this totality into act, then it is just as though the norm and its violation were presented to us simultaneously.

The transcending of contradictions no longer, henceforth, comes from outside: communism is no longer an Utopia or a moral system, but the expression of a real movement.

(c) The birth of a need. This real movement is experienced subjectively by a social class as a need. This can be clearly seen in the industrial revolts of the silk-workers of Lyons, the Chartists in England, the Silesian weavers, and later the Paris rising in June 1848.

Marxism is the theoretical expression of this coincidence of a concrete project and a real need, of scientific socialism and the working-class movement.

It no longer has a moral character; it is no longer an ideal divorced from life, but is instead fundamentally the development of a praxis.

It was in this sense that Marx could write in *The Holy Family*: 'Communists preach no ethical system.' Marx was inflexible in his opposition to Weitling, who justified the communist attitude by moral reasons, and to the Utopians, who adopted a moral point of view. 'Morality,' he wrote in *The Holy Family*, 'in the sense of the morality which justifies itself by reference to an ideal value is simply impotence put into action.'

In point of fact every moral system has, so far, been an alienation based on the concept of the double man, that is of alienated man, on the concept of a dual nature in man.

'For us,' wrote Marx again, 'communism is not a stable state which is to be established, an *ideal* to which reality will have to adjust itself. We call communism the *real* movement which abolishes the present state of things. The conditions of this movement result from the premises now in existence' (*The German Ideology*, p. 48).

History is nothing but the generation of man by man, through the medium of social labour.

Within this generation, however, there are produced, as a result of the division of labour and of private ownership, the alienations which lie at the root of class struggles and antagonisms.

Thus at the present time, the meaning of history (and by that I do not mean some theological necessity, some providence or inevitable destiny, but the only meaning that we can by our free choice attribute to history and our own life) is the struggle of the proletariat, of the class, that is, which suffers the most profoundly de-humanising consequences of alienation: of an alienation which is not merely ideological illusion but also the objective dehumanisation resulting from alienation of labour.

In virtue of that, this class contains within itself, at a time when a global organisation of needs, resources, and hopes has become possible, the project of and the demand for a total disalienation, the project of total man.

The formation of this project does not derive from any millenarist illusion of realising a city of God, a city of the Sun upon earth. This project constitutes the horizon of our labour, our culture, and our fight.

This project of total man, the project, that is, of a completely interiorised society, of a completely disalienated individual (consciously containing society within himself in the form of culture and the feeling of his own responsibility)—is this project, too, an Utopia?

Does this humanism take us back again to a moral socialism?

Can total man be a supreme value and an ultimate end without being a transcendent ideal?

Or can there, then, be a non-alienated form of transcendence?

So far, every ethic has been an alienation, because it has been founded on the duality of being and ideal.

Is some other dualism possible?

There is the alienated dualism of transcendence, and there

is the dualism in the eyes of which the transcendent is the tragic side of immanent development.

From this second point of view, transcendence is not a severance but a deeper and fuller development: to put it more exactly it is a dialectical supersession.

The problem lies in thinking of the transcendent otherwise than as a category of exteriority; unless one can do this transcendence is simply another name for alienation, and such a God is rightly called an idol.

Does this mean that a non-alienated conception of transcendence is necessarily negative: is it the experience of a lack, of a tension?

Negation is, no doubt, the first picture—the first analogue —we form of such transcendence.

The demand that governs all scientific development, the demand for a systematic whole and for total intelligibility, is and will always be a postulate that no experiment can verify but which is the very condition of all experiment.

The demand that governs all ethical development, the demand for total man, is of the same order; for nothing is ever promised to the atheists we are. Nobody is waiting for us.

Is transcendence, then, always and necessarily the experience of an absence and not of a presence? We must always, it is true, resist the mystical and mystifying temptation of converting a need into a presence; nevertheless, when we consider the movement that constantly leads us to create, in anguish and peril, a higher reality, we can become conscious of it as constituting what is our most profound reality, as the reality which constitutes creative man.

This reality, we have already seen, is identified with the presence in ourselves of others, of the totality of others, a presence which cannot be lived as an experience of exteriority: the other and my own self are one. This otherness is not exteriority, since I can decide to accept as governing my own decision the will which was at first in opposition to me.

The tension between myself and the other, between the

finite and the infinite (that is, between the I and the totality of others) makes possible the reciprocal involvement of transcendence and immanence. Already, for Fichte, the finite I was an absolute, only because it included in itself, in its activity, this affirmation of finite and infinite which Spinozist dogmatism projected outside it into being.

We can therefore define transcendence by emptying it of all the meaning which it contains only in virtue of an obsolete conception of the world.

To investigate the dimension of transcendence, conceived not as an attribute to God but as a dimension of man, is not to start from something which exists in our world in a vain attempt to prove the existence of what can exist only in another world: it is simply to investigate all the dimensions of human reality.

When I love a human being, I make a wager—I put my money on that being—in a way that goes beyond all his acts. The closest image, then, we can form of this transcendence is perhaps that of the love, of the strictly human love, through which we learn to see, or rather to postulate, in the loved being, a quality which shares no common measure with the contents of his acts.

In an enthralling passage on St John of the Cross, Aragon, in *Le Fou d'Elsa*, gives us a poetic approximation of Pascal's wager, which, at the strictly human level of love, defines transcendence.

The encounter with the transcendent, or rather the emergence of transcendence, is not a privileged experience, nor is there in it anything theological or religious. It is not an interruption of the natural order by a supernatural intervention; it is the commonest, the specific, human experience: the experience of creation.

Transcendence is a dimension of ordinary life. It is attested by the continual possibility of choosing to live and die for others. This conscious, voluntary, free choice defines us as man, cut off from animality and alienation.

It is through this detachment from nature and the given, which begins with work and attains its highest expression when death becomes no longer simply the revenge of the species on the individual but the individual's gift of love to the whole of mankind, it is through this that a transcendental, and that values, are continually being born.

If we accept this concept, we take as our starting point in moral criticism not a solitary cogito but praxis—we realise, that is, that man begins with labour, that this labour is always social, that labour, inasmuch as it goes beyond what is given to us, constitutes the first category of ethics, and that consciousness of self is subordinate to communication with others: thus, the concept enables us to emancipate ourselves from individualism while at the same time respecting the autonomy of consciousness.

It helps us to understand that man is a creator, that he is his own creator, and it provides us with the means of overcoming alienation, which is the opposite of creation—of overcoming it for all of us: it enables us, that is, to base an indivisibly social and personal ethic not simply on its theoretical justification but on its practical realisation: an ethic whose ultimate end creates the conditions which will make it possible for every man to become effectively a man, that is to say a creator.

It was in this sense that Maxim Gorky admirably defined our concept, when he said that for communists aesthetics is the ethics of the future.

CHAPTER FOUR

Marxism and Religion

*

In Marxism, atheism is a consequence of humanism and an aspect of the fight against dogmatism.

It is this that distinguishes it from earlier forms of atheism.

Eighteenth-century atheism is essentially *political*. In their unavoidable fight against the social and political institutions inherited from the past, the materialist philosophers and the Encyclopaedists came up against a Church which was at that time an aspect of the State and which sanctioned despotism by 'divine right'. Their struggle against religion was a struggle to win freedom from tyranny. Baron d'Holbach, in concluding his *Le Christianisme dévoilé*, emphasises the political character of his essay in criticism. 'Everything that has so far been said shows with unmistakable clarity that the Christian religion runs counter to the political health and well-being of nations.' 'Religion is the art of making men drunk with ecstasy in order to divert their attention from the evils heaped upon them here below by those who govern them.'

Similarly, Meslier writes: 'Ignorance and fear, these are the two king-pins of all religion . . . The aim of those who first gave laws to peoples was to dominate them: the easiest way to do so was to frighten them and prevent them from using their minds . . . The more one thinks about religious dogmas and principles, the stronger is one's conviction that their only aim is to benefit tyrants and priests.'

This atheism played an eminently progressive political part in the destruction of feudal relationships and absolute monarchy, by unmasking the political and social use of religion by the Ancien Régime. In that lies its greatness. Its limitation is that it saw in religion nothing but an arbitrary invention, without asking either what human needs it met or what human values had been created in this religious form.

Nineteenth-century atheism (apart from Marxism) was on the whole 'scientist'. It opposed religious ideology as being a pre-scientific or non-scientific explanation of the world. This atheism, too, played a positive part by driving from the field all the attempts to contain God in the provisional insufficiencies of knowledge, all the superstitions that nourish the appetite for mystery, the readiness to accept man's impotence and welcome the miraculous. And once again, its limitation was that it was exclusively negative. The most striking example of this is Auguste Comte's 'law of the three states'. According to Comte, human thought 'is obliged, both in the individual and in the species, to pass through three successive states: theological, metaphysical and positive.' To reduce the scientific spirit to positivism is not only to claim that man is barred from raising the problems of ends and meaning; it is also to justify this prohibition in virtue of an impoverished and alienated conception of science as something confined to 'facts' and the establishment of constant relations between them. Philosophy, with theology and metaphysics, is bundled into the same barrow-load of illusions devoid of content.

Marxist atheism, which is also twentieth-century atheism, is essentially *humanist*. It starts, not from a negation, but from an affirmation: it affirms the autonomy of man and it involves as a consequence the rejection of every attempt to rob man of his creative and self-creative power.

In his *Economic and Philosophic Manuscripts of 1844* we already find Marx emphasising this aspect: 'Atheism . . . is no longer meaningful, for atheism is a negation of God and seeks to assert by this negation the existence of man. Socialism no longer requires such a roundabout method . . . it is positive human self-consciousness' (in *Early Writings*, p. 167). In other words humanism is no more to be defined by the negation of religion (and so still by relationship to religion) than communism is to be defined as the negation of private ownership (and so still by its relationship to the latter).

There can be no doubt but that Marxist atheism is the heir of the battles fought for the emancipation of man and his thought by eighteenth- and nineteenth-century atheism. It is the heir, too, of the humanism of Fichte and Hegel, which restores to man the powers traditionally alienated in God; the heir, again, of Feuerbach's humanism which sets itself up against a religion which cuts man off from what is best in him by projecting his hopes and virtues into God. The young Marx summed up this humanist heritage in the foreword to his doctoral thesis in 1841: 'Philosophy adopts as its own, Prometheus' profession of faith: "I hate all the gods!" It raises that cry against all the gods of heaven and earth that do not recognise man's consciousness as the supreme deity. It brooks no rival.'

What characterises specifically Marxist atheism is that, unlike its predecessors, it does not regard religion simply as a lie fabricated by despots or as a pure and simple illusion born of ignorance.

Marx and Engels studied the problem of what human needs were, in some mystified way, met by religions. They are, Marx observed, at once a *reflection* of a real distress and a *protest* against it.

In so far as it is a *reflection* of man's impotence and distress, religion is seen to be an ideology that both explains and justifies the existing order. Thus it is used, more or less constantly, as a decisive weapon which makes it possible to teach the masses that the established order is willed by God and that, as obedient and submissive subjects, they should resign themselves to it. The doctrine of original sin has been used for this purpose. In his *City of God*, St Augustine wrote: 'God introduced slavery into the world as a punishment for original sin: to seek, therefore, to abolish slavery would be to rebel against the will of God.' The Church has constantly sanctioned all forms of class domination as being willed by God —slavery, serfdom, wage-earning—and the most recent restatements of her 'social teaching' still retain this basic orientation. Karl Marx summed up this undeniable historical fact in his succinct phrase, 'Religion is the opium of the people.'

Accompanying, however, the element of *reflection*, there is also that of *protest*. This latter is the element of religion in virtue of which it is not simply an ideology—the quest for an explanation of unhappiness and helplessness—but is an attempt to find a *way out* from unhappiness: in other words, it is no longer just a way of thinking, but a way of *acting*: no longer an ideology but a faith, a way of confronting the world and behaving in it.

Here we meet phenomena of great complexity. This faith is expressed in a very different way in history.

Marxists do not treat 'religion' in general in a metaphysical and idealist way, but as historians and materialists. They try to find out how, in historical conditions that have to be scientifically analysed in each case, faith can play a positive and progressive part.

This simply means that even if the well-known phrase 'Religion is the opium of the people' corresponds to an undeniable historical fact, and one that is very largely confirmed even today, the Marxist concept of religion cannot be reduced to that phrase.

The thesis that religion *as such*, at all times and in all places, diverts man from action, from working and fighting, is a flagrant contradiction of historical reality.

Engels analysed two different examples of the role of faith in history: in his studies of primitive Christianity, he shows how this religious faith (before it assumed the form of an ideology and a conservative institution, in the hands of the ruling power, with Constantine) was a protest, but an *im-*

potent protest. He shows how these first Christian communities dreamed of an Apocalypse: that is to say, in most concrete terms, they dreamed of the destruction of the dominance of Rome which was crushing them. He speaks of this primitive Christianity as a 'revolutionary element': which is evident enough, if one considers that public authority was sufficiently alarmed by it to organise ferocious repressive counter-measures—and that not simply for religious reasons, since there was a proliferation of other alien cults which were tolerated. Engels comments on 'the faith of these first militant communities,' just as Lenin in *The State and Revolution* commented on the 'democratic revolutionary spirit of primitive Christianity' (*Collected Works*, Vol. 21, New York, 1932, p. 184). Those communities were unable, however, to effect their revolution, because there was at that time no social force which could take over the collapsing world of Rome and lead it into a progressive future: and the Christian ideology itself reflected the historical impotence of slave-revolts. So marked was this that the passionate longing for change was transformed into a dream; it became the expectation of the fulfilment of a promise, and, ultimately, an ideology of escape, of flight, of resignation, which postponed to another world what could not be realised in this world. This compensation in heaven, built up into an ideology, with an admixture of neo-platonic traditions, was one day to become a marvellous opium; and, from Constantine until our own day, the ruling power has been able to make extensive use of that opium to ensure the acceptance of suffering in this world in expectation of what is promised in the next.

The essential truth of Engel's analysis has been confirmed by researches into Christian origins, and the accompanying discoveries, in which remarkable progress has been made, in particular since the first finding of the Dead Sea Scrolls in 1947.

It would appear that from the very beginning we must

distinguish two currents in the elements that make up the extremely complex syncretism of Christianity, the Judaeo-Christian current and the Helleno-Christian.

The former, which was dominant in the Church of Jerusalem, appeared as an offshoot of the Jewish religious movements of the first century BC. These were often revolutionary in inspiration: they were movements of popular national liberation directed against foreign rulers, Babylonian and Assyrian in earlier times and later Seleucid and Roman. They were for the most part expressed in a messianic prophetism.

This prophetism was a protest not only against the political and religious dominance of the foreigner, but also against the oppression of the controlling classes, the higher Jewish priesthood (the Sadducees, for example), who mostly collaborated with the occupying power.

The tactics of these socially revolutionary movements were those of non-violence, of exemplary purity, of preaching. The Essene sects practised common ownership and non-violence. That they had a great influence on the first Christian communists in Jerusalem is attested by numerous episodes in the Gospels and the Acts of the Apostles.

Side by side, however, with this waiting upon the realisation of the Kingdom, there was also the violent activity of the Zealots. We find evidence of this in other passages in the synoptic gospels: the sack of the Temple, the trial of Christ, who was condemned for having been proclaimed 'King of the Jews'.

This current appears to have contributed to making Christianity a factor that worked for the break-up of the power of Rome. There was revolutionary significance in many of its manifestations: in the hostility to the cult of the emperor, in the refusal to be associated with it, and, still more, in the forbidding of Christians to serve in the imperial army at a time when recruiting was becoming more and more difficult and the Christian population was increasing daily: a ban that was to persist until the fourth century. Thus in the person of Christ, magnified by the collective imagination of the first Christians and accepted as the heir of numerous similar Messiahs (such as the Essene 'Teacher of Righteousness' who was put to death by Hyrcanus II in the first century AD), there was an undeniable revolutionary aspect. This derives from a whole national, popular, tradition which attains in it a universal extension, for it burst out from the national framework in which it had been contained when the synthesis with Hellenism was effected in the teaching of St Paul, who refused to address himself only to the circumcised.

The theme of the role of the 'Just Man' in the unfolding of history was frequently to reappear in Christian tradition. It was to underlie the controversy between St Augustine and Pelagius, the former accepting the neo-platonic hellenic tradition and defending the proposition of predestination and submission to the divine order, and the latter refusing to admit the transmission by generation of original sin and instead attributing to man's activity its full value.

This vindication of justice and of man's struggle will be found again in Thomas Münzer, at a breaking-point in history when new social forces emerged in the sixteenth century; and we see it looming up in our own day at a new stage in history, when the working class is shattering the structures of the older world and so creating the conditions for a renascence, within Christianity, of the human values of action and combat.

This Judaeo-Christian current was soon absorbed, and eventually almost completely submerged, by the Helleno-Christian current.

This latter was at first the dominant current in the churches of Asia Minor, the East, and Greece. It was the expression of a desire to escape from the world, and to secure individual salvation guaranteed by faith in Christ, the Pauline 'Master'. It derived from the break-up of the 'guardian deity' religions of Greece, which assured man's salvation within the framework of the ancient city state. Its development kept in step with the transformation of the Greek world into a Hellenistic world, soon to be dominated by the Roman empire. With the collapse of the city state, and the abandonment of the individual to his own isolation, the Helleno-Christian current offered the road to individual salvation in an escape into the hereafter.

Engels gives us another example from history in which, in another encounter of social forces, faith assumed another significance. In the sixteenth century, with the emergence of new social forces, faith takes on a militant form and, with Thomas Münzer, led to an armed rising. These insurgent peasants wished to see the will of God 'done on earth as it is in heaven', and they proposed to contribute to this victory by taking up arms. The insurgents, writes Engels, wanted 'the egalitarian conditions of primitive Christianity to be accepted as normal for civil society. From the equality of men before God they deduced civil equality and, to some degree already, equality of possessions' (cf. *The Peasant War in Germany*, trans. M. J. Olgin, London, 1927, p. 54). He recalls and quotes the premises underlying the agitation of Thomas Münzer, the theologian of the revolution. 'Heaven, he taught, was to be sought in this life, not beyond; and it was the task of believers to establish Heaven, the Kingdom of God, here on earth' (*Ibid*, pp. 65-6). For Münzer, he adds, 'The Kingdom of God was a society without class differences, without private property, and without super-imposed state powers opposed to the members of society' (*Ibid*, p. 67). When the insurrection broke out in the autumn of 1513, the banner carried by the insurgents of the 'Bundschuh' bore the legend 'Lord, uphold thy divine justice' (*Ibid*, p. 80).

One of the greatest merits of Maurice Thorez was that he was the first in the international communist movement to combat the tendencies to simplify and narrow down the Marxist concept of religion, which, in France, was often

contaminated by bourgeois anti-clericalism and by the reduction of Marx's premises to those of the eighteenth century.

In his report, dated 26th October 1937, to the Assembly of
party representatives at the Palais de la Mutualité and en-
titled 'Communists and Catholics: the outstretched hand'
(*Oeuvres*, Vol. 14, pp. 159-81), Thorez referred to the well-
known passage in Engels, in which he speaks of the points
of contact between the history of primitive Christianity and
the modern workers' movement, and went on to say: 'The
philosophical materialism of communists is removed from
the religious faith of Catholics. Nevertheless, whatever the
opposition between their doctrinal concepts, it is impossible
not to distinguish in both the same warm-hearted ardour to
try to satisfy men's age-old aspirations for a better life:

' "The promise of a redeemer sheds a glow on the first
page of human history," says the Catholic.'

' "The hope of a universal city, reconciled in labour and
love maintains the effort of the proletarians who fight for
the happiness of all men," says the Communist.'

It was thus that Maurice Thorez extracted from the crimes
of *the institution* and the mystifications of the *ideology* the store
of warm-hearted ardour that can, in certain determined
historical conditions, be found in faith; and so, to the great
indignation of those whom he was later to describe as 'the
fanatical bigots who raise the cry of "Unity but no priests",'
he commented, in the same address (to quote his actual
words), on 'the progressive role of Christianity.' Of this he
distinguished, in past history, two aspects:

the progressive role it has played in its fight to make human
relationships more just and more peaceful.

the progressive role it has played in its contribution to
culture and the arts.

The French Communist Party has remained true to this
line.

On 13th March 1966, when the Central Committee had
finished its work on these problems, Waldeck-Rochet first

recalled the constant elements in Marxist policy in relation
to religion, as follows:

on the *historical* plane, a class war against the factual solidarity of religious institutions and the reactionary forces
which they sanction and justify.

on the *philosophical* plane, an ideological war against every
tendency to gloss over the opposition between materialist
philosophy and the principle on which every religion is based.

He then went on to give a definition of sectarianism which
is of cardinal importance for the future of dialogue and co-
operation between Christians and Marxists: 'We reject,' he
said, 'every limited, sectarian, interpretation of the religious
fact . . . We do not form our impression of religious thought
by looking at it from one side only, noting in it only that
aspect by which it is an obstacle to human progress and a
brake on it.'

What is of capital importance in what Waldeck-Rochet
said is that, in contrast with all earlier forms of atheism,
Marxism can integrate all the human aspirations which are
to be found, in a mystified form, among believers.

*

By bringing out what, in religion, is a *reflection* of real distress
and what is a *protest* against it, Marx suggests a method for
analysing the real human content which is mystified in the
form of religion: the method is, starting from an examination
of from what real social relationships the imaginative *reflection*
is formed and the *protest* born, to study at the same time in
each particular historical case the *active* phase of the demand
to go beyond these relationships (even if this demand is mis-
directed, diverted from the point at which it should be
applied socially and militantly and aimed at the heaven of
personal salvation).

Marx himself embarked on this analysis as early as 1844
in *The Jewish Question*. In this series of articles he raised the
problem of the human 'core' of religions, his starting point

115

being a criticism of Bruno Bauer's views on the emancipation of the Jews.

Marx approves and praises Bauer's initial approach, which he sums up as follows: 'As soon as Jew and Christian come to see in their respective religions nothing more than stages in the development of the human mind—snake skins which have been cast off by history and man as the snake who clothed himself in them—they will no longer find themselves in religious opposition, but in a purely critical, scientific and human relationship' (in *Early Writings*, p. 5).

He then goes on to a fundamental criticism of Bauer's analysis of the conditions for Jewish emancipation. 'It was by no means sufficient to ask: Who should emancipate? Who should be emancipated? The critic should ask a third question: What kind of emancipation is involved?' (*Ibid*, p. 7).

Lacking critical sense, Bauer 'confuses political emancipation and universal human emancipation' (*Ibid*, p. 8).

With Bauer, Marx accepts the Hegelian thesis that the different religions are no more than 'different degrees of the development of the human mind, "snake-skins sloughed by man"' (p. 5).

With Bauer, Marx accepts Feuerbach's thesis that religion is the recognition of man in a roundabout way, through a mediation, through a mediator (p. 11), and that it is because of that that it is an alienation.

In opposition, however, to Bauer, and carrying the criticism of religion very much further than did Hegel and Feuerbach, Marx discloses the roots of religious alienation in the real world of history.

He reproaches Bauer for not having made a 'radical' criticism, a criticism, that is, which gets right down to the roots; the concrete man.

'Political emancipation represents a great progress. It is not the final force in human emancipation' (p. 10). In fact, by abolishing privilege and proclaiming political equality, the French Revolution (bourgeois democracy in general) allowed the survival, outside the sphere of the State, of economic inequalities, with the exploitation and oppression they produce.

In such a (bourgeois democratic) State, man will continue to live a *double* life, a life of heaven and a life of earth.

This division of man between his life which is abandoned to the jungles of capitalism and his illusory life as an 'abstract citizen' of an abstract community in which he finds ersatz 'species-being', is characteristic of both political and religious alienation.

Marx explains in *Capital* that the Christian religion is particularly adapted to the requirements of an individualist commercial society, in which man, isolated as an individual, looks for a heavenly compensation for this solitude in 'the cult of the abstract man . . . The religious complement which is most suited' to societies of this type. It is this that Marx, in a passage in which he sums up the main theses of historical materialism, calls the '*earthly nucleus* of the cloudy concepts of religions'.

In the democratic bourgeois state we find a secularised expression of this split-up of man: it expresses 'in a human and secular form, in its political reality, the human basis of which Christianity is the transcendental expression' (*The Jewish Question*, in *Early Writings*, p. 16). In this democratic bourgeois state, 'the human core of religion is realised in a profane manner' (*Ibid*, p. 17). It is there realised with all its illusions.

With all its illusions, because, says Marx in *The Jewish Question*, 'the existence of religion is the existence of a deficiency' (*Ibid*, p. 9), of a lack, which is sanctioned by the bourgeois democratic state. What happens is that man, abandoned to the self-centred isolation of the jungle of the commercial economy, and dominated by alien forces which threaten and crush him, lives the 'split-up' which characterises religious life: in his real life he is an individual, cut off from properly human life, which, in Marx's words, is the life of a 'species-being'; and he seeks a heavenly compensation for this lack, this shortcoming. His 'species-life', which is his properly human life (as opposed to the self-centred individualism entailed by capitalism and, more generally, by the commercial economy), he projects into heaven, where love reigns and man recognises himself as a species-being (living and dying for the whole of mankind): But this, as Marx says, he does in a roundabout way, through a mediator, Christ—not, that is, in real life, but in an 'illusory compensation', by an alienation.

Thus, in every commercial society,[1] religion expresses everything that is lacking in this world, 'its solemn complement, its general basis of consolation and justification. It is the fantastic realisation of the human being, inasmuch as the human being possesses no true reality' (Marx, *Critique of Hegel's Philosophy of Right*, in *Early Writings*, p. 43).

The bourgeois democratic state sanctions this split: that of the individual's real life in civil society (as Hegel and the young Marx said) and of the 'citizen's' abstract life in a community in which he exercises absolute sovereignty. 'It can dispense with religion, because in this case the human core of religion is realised in a profane manner' (*Early Writings*, p. 17).

Parting company with Bauer, Marx shows that this political emancipation, however, is not the universal human emancipation which he defines at the end of his *The Jewish Question*. This is effected when 'the conflict between the individual, sensuous existence of man and his species-existence is abolished' (*Ibid*, p. 40). 'Political emancipation is a reduction of man, on the one hand to a member of civil society, an inde-

---

[1] I am referring here to the commercial societies of which Christianity, Marx says, is the most suitable complement. Were it my intention to write a history of *the religions*, it would be necessary, as Marx suggests, to study the conditions in which 'the closeness of men's relations either with one another, or with nature are ideally reflected in the ancient *national religions*.'

pendent and egotistic individual, and on the other hand to a citizen, to a *moral person*.

'Human emancipation will be complete only when man . . . has recognised and organised his own powers as social powers so that he no longer separates this social power from himself as political power' (*Ibid*, p. 31).

From this historical point of view the concepts of humanism and of religion which we find in Marx take on their true materialist and dialectical significance.

Religions are born, live, and die in determined historical conditions. To confine ourselves to the example of Christianity, Marx, we have seen, showed in *Capital* how it was particularly well adapted to a commercial economy in which man is split up into a self-centred individual in his real life, and a 'moral person' in the heavenly compensation he seeks for the lack of species-life. What is significant in this is the Kantian abstraction of the 'citizen' who postulates the 'ideal' of a 'kingdom of ends', in which every 'person' must be treated as an end and never as a means, at the very moment when the universalisation of the laws of capitalism, with its rivalries and class exploitations, makes every man into a means and every object into a commodity.

The emancipation of the whole man, of which Marx speaks at the end of *The Jewish Question* (*Early Writings*, p. 40), abolishes conflict between man's individual and sensuous life and his species-life, and so ends the divorce between the real individual and the ideal 'person'. In a society in which there is no longer any division into classes, the individual shares fully in all mankind's earlier conquests, through his culture, and in the continued and conscious creation of mankind by itself, through his personal responsibility towards the whole, his real (and not illusory) solidarity with all, and his certain knowledge that there is no limit to the creative power of men.

What happens to religion, then? As religion, it disappears; and what Marx, as early as the stage of political emancipation (in the bourgeois democratic state) called its 'human core' is realised in a secular way; it is now realised, that is, not in an illusory and abstract form, which leaves religious alienation intact, but in a real and practical form.

What was this human core? It was, in the first place, as Marx emphasized, the 'lack', the 'deficiency', in which can be seen in the isolated individual—fragmented and mutilated by the commercial economy—the absence of the species-life, the specifically human life, the life, that is, which shares in all that has been won in history by mankind. Religion is both a *reflection* of this lack, this deficiency, and a *revolt* against it, even if the revolt remains purely subjective. Primitive Christianity was not a slave-revolution but a slave-religion. This does not prevent Engels, after condemning 'the baldly rationalist point of view' according to which 'one type of superstition is just as foolish as another' (*On Religion*, p. 313) from seeing in Christianity 'a completely new phase in the evolution of religion, destined to become one of the most revolutionary elements in the history of the human mind' (*Ibid*, p. 322). Emphasising the element of 'protest', Engels draws a parallel with socialism and adds that in primitive Christianity 'there is the feeling that man is fighting against a whole world and that he will emerge as the victor from that fight: a militant ardour and a certainty of winning which have completely disappeared in the Christians of our own day and are to be found only at the opposite pole of society, in the socialists' (p. 323). Such is the first aspect of this human core, this consciousness of a lack and this protest against it: even if the protest sometimes takes a purely moral utopian, and mythical, form.

This 'human core' in Christianity is not confined to the 'protest' against what man lacks. What man, what the alienated individual lacks in the world of commodities, is the possibility of living his species-life, as the young Marx said; and it is to this that religious alienation provides an answer by promising that this irrepressible aspiration is indeed satisfied, but in another world, in a boundless community in which a law of love reigns supreme.

Here we have another central aspect of the 'human core' of Christianity, which gives a mystified answer to a real question, an illusory satisfaction to an authentic demand.

Herein, too, we have 'a common denominator', on the strictly human plane, between Christians and communists. This was a point forcibly emphasised by Maurice Thorez as it was, earlier, by Engels (cf. above, p. 114).

Every Marxist who does not ludicrously impoverish dialectical materialism and the concept of man which derives from it, must necessarily rediscover this thesis. Thus, Aragon, for example, criticising his own earlier ideas, in which 'the primitive materialist I then was condemned the Christian supernatural,' wrote (from hiding in occupied France), 'The relation which is born from the negation of the real by the supernatural is essentially ethical in character, and the supernatural is always the materialisation of a moral symbol which is violently in opposition to the ethic of the world from the midst of which it arises.' He commented on 'the generous, human element in this divine faith . . . which is a concept of man that the communist and the Christian can have, but never the Nazi' (*De l'exactitude historique en poésie*).

Aragon, too, tries to define this 'common denominator' in certain aspects of our 'concept of man'. He finds in St John of the Cross the highest expression of love, and relates it to its 'human core':

John of the Cross, you are but the name the Christian gives
to all who in their love
write their own doom.
And I, as you whose passion knows no bourne,
I pass by the bed on which, beyond the love of God, you mourn.
For from this world must come the answer to the question that is me:
And he who casts away this world is lost: he finds,
As he cuts short his road,

but the dizzy cliff that runs beside the path:
For of this world is the answer,
Of this world the love and the high deed
Of this man John, who bears the name of the Cross.

(*Le Fou d'Elsa*, p. 355.)

The Marxist concept of alienation, therefore, in no way leads to a method of *reducing* man and his mind to the historical, economic and social conditions in which they are born, nor to a *deductive* method which starts with those conditions.

For Marx and Marxists, alienation is not a moral but an historical category: the subjective contradictions within man are not separable from his social contradictions. If we consider man independently of society, alienation is necessarily treated in an abstract way, whereas for Marx, as a materialist, alienation is not simply a theory based on illusion, but is in the first place alienation from real life and, with that as its starting point, it entails for him the study of the illusions which this fundamental alienation produces.

In our own day, the building up of socialism in numerous countries enables us to develop more deeply Marx's teaching, in this as in all other spheres.

In *Capital*, Marx not only eliminated from the notion of alienation (and both the word and the concept are to be found in *Capital*) all that is contained of idealist speculation in Hegel and of metaphysical anthropology in Feuerbach, but also studied scientifically a particular form of it to which he gave the name of 'the fetishism of commodities'.

He showed that in a capitalist régime the principal source of alienation is the exploitation of man by man, with all the machinery for the crushing of man which is entailed by this class antagonism and class domination. From this it follows that the inauguration of socialism by putting an end, through collective ownership of the means of production, to the fundamental phenomenon of class exploitation, tears up the strongest roots of man's present alienation.

To conclude, however, that this means that with the coming of socialism all possibility of alienation is removed, would be to forget in the first place that Marx holds that, quite apart from specifically capitalist class relationships and even from the various forms of division of society into classes, the 'fetishism of commodities' derives from these commodity relationships themselves. Thus, this fetishism is found even before the appearance of slavery, with the birth of the first commodity relationships; and it will continue to have an objective foundation so long as a profit economy remains, so long as the law of value still operates as the accompaniment of commodity relationships, profoundly transformed though they may be in the conditions of a socialist régime. Inter-human relations will still not be 'transparent' since they will pass through the mediation of commodity production.

Alienation, moreover, has other social roots, in particular those that are linked with the existence of the State. Here again, the new class relations which come in with socialism will no longer, it is true, necessarily produce the forms of 'bureaucracy' which are closely connected with class privilege and are characteristic of the machinery of State in a capitalist régime; nevertheless, the fact that the State must necessarily still exist during the building up first of socialism and then of communism, produces (as historical experience has shown) specific forms of bureaucracy, with all that entails for the individual's attitude towards the socialist State.

To deny the possibility and the reality of certain forms of alienation in a socialist régime, not only makes it impossible to explain the persistence of the phenomenon of religion, by denying the existence of the objective conditions of its development and treating it as no more than a survival: it is also to adopt an apologetic attitude towards the building up of socialism which hinders its development; it is to foster what can truly be called 'socialist irrealism' in art and ethics, and to rob the building up of socialism of the leaven provided by the critical spirit.

Marx's materialist analysis was never the victim of such illusions. 'The religious reflection of the real world can, in any case, only then finally vanish when the practical relations of every-day life offer to man none but *perfectly intelligible and reasonable relations with regard to his fellow-men and to nature*' (*Capital*, Vol. I, p. 79).

This concept of transparent and reasonable relations with his fellow-men *and with nature* enables us to see more deeply into the Marxist concept of the roots of religion. Nothing can be perfectly 'transparent and reasonable' for man unless he has made, constructed, created it himself. That is why mathematics, for example, has always been regarded as a model of intelligibility.

Now, while Marx was constantly showing that man, through labour (in its specifically human form) is his own creator, and while on countless occasions he pointed out that man creates his own history, he always combated the illusion that man is also the creator of nature, or even the arbitrary creator of a human history which does not have to take into account the necessities of nature, and even those of this 'second nature' (humanised, indeed, but none the less objective) which man has moulded in the actual course of his history.

In his *Critique of the Gotha Programme*, Marx comments ironically on 'the supernatural creative power' attributed to human labour by economists who pass over the fact that 'labour depends on nature' and that 'it is only in so far as man treats nature as belonging to him' that his labour becomes a source of wealth (in *Selected Works*, p. 319). This idealist mystification has a class character: it serves to mask the very principle of capitalist exploitation: to become the owner of the object is to enslave the subject.

Marx's materialist position is accordingly perfectly clear: labour is the creative act which creates *not nature*, but man and his history in his encounter with nature.

Thus, before the division of society into classes, before even the appearance of relations of production, and quite apart from what Lenin calls the 'social roots of religion', there is in the consciousness of men a reflection (based on fantasy) of external powers. 'In the beginnings of history,' says Engels, 'it was the forces of nature which were first so reflected' (*Anti-Dühring*, p. 353); and later he was to add (in his letter to Conrad Schmidt dated 27 October, 1890) that it would be 'pedantic to try to find economic causes' for these first religious representations.

Side by side, then, with the social roots, there are (as Lenin said) other roots, in religion as in idealism, which spring from the very movement of knowledge—gnoseological roots. Lenin emphasises that knowledge 'is not a *reflection* in a mirror but a complex *act* . . . which includes the possibility of an imaginative flight from life; and, even more, it includes the possibility of a transformation of the abstract concept into an imaginative fantasy (which ultimately=God). For even in the most elementary generalisation there is a certain imaginative content. And vice versa it is absurd to deny the role of imagination even in the most exact science'.

Here Lenin forcibly restates one of the major themes in the Marxist theory of knowledge. Marx, we have seen, showed that it was from labour that was born every form of specifically human activity, whether in technology, in religion or in art, all of which are forms of activity that exist in no other animal species. Now, what characterises specifically human labour is that its end pre-exists in the consciousness of man and constitutes the law which guides his action. It is this active presence of the future, this anticipation, this project, which is characteristic of man. This imaginative or conceptual projection lies at the root of all human activity.

The emphasis laid on the 'active side' of knowledge is one particular case of this.

A project is an anticipation of the real. Starting from conditions in which it is born, and as a function of them, consciousness projects its own ends. This projection is initially imaginative and mythical. Even when mythical, the project is a way of severing oneself from the immediate given, of transcending it, and anticipating the real, either in order to justify the existing order (reflection), or in order to rebel against it (protest) and endeavour to change it.

Religion is a project by man, but a mystified project.

'In primitive man,' writes Henri Wallon (*De L'acte à la pensée*, pp. 106-8), 'the attempt to explain the visible by the invisible is not a sort of aberration that leads him away from the real . . . It is the condition indispensable to every intellectual effort, if its aim is to transcend the data provided by experience that is simply lived, and, to discover, behind the effects in which our activity is involved, the causes from which they result, and from which it will be possible to derive procedures enabling us to act upon them other than by reacting to them immediately through sensori-motor means alone. Thus there is a similarity of function in both myth and science: they are both the world of causes, underlying and involved in the world of sensible effects.'

Ritual is a first technique, as myth is a first science. 'On the day when man's activity was guided in the satisfaction of his needs, by something other than his automations, on the day when it was subordinated to rituals that were distinct from the thing itself, when it sought to give reality to images that transcended its sensible appearances, on that day there began the great speculative adventure' (*Ibid*, p. 115) by which our species has been qualitatively differentiated from the animal kingdom.

'The occult,' Wallon goes on to say (p. 115), 'is a category or rather the matrix of categories through the medium of which man has endeavoured, in order to act upon the universe, to conceptualise and know it, taking it as being distinct from the simple situations which belong to crude immediate experience, assuming it to possess a deeper reality than is found in ephemeral appearances, looking in it for something other than a mere occasion for his own activities (whether impromptu or the fruit of habit), attributing to it constancy of principles, and identifying it with lasting powers, influences that have to be submitted to or dominated, and reasons that can be foreseen with certainty.'

We would be greatly mistaken in concluding that this genetic analysis of knowledge tends to obliterate the frontier between concept and myth, science and religion.

Wallon brings out in the different stages of the child's development, the complex dialectic by which the fusion of thought and reality is effected in a series of hypotheses which are shown to be untrue and operations which have to be corrected. Thought is defined as reflection, but the reflection is not present for us at the beginning; it is built up actively and progressively.

This conception leaves no room either for idealism, or for agnosticism, but involves a dialectical materialism 'which is not belief in an immediate identity between the crude impression things make on us and their essence, but is, on the contrary, the certainty that there is progress and change in what we know and that, at every period, this is a witness to the laws and structures that our technical advances enable us to discover and bring into action in nature' (pp. 120-1).

Henri Wallon has studied in minute detail the transition from immediate practical understanding to that which uses rituals and myths as a starting point for its development into science.

Knowledge of the world progresses dialectically by overcoming the contradictions between the ever wider approximations of techniques and hypotheses and the recalcitrance of a reality which is not immediately identical with the image we form of it, and only gradually lends itself to the techniques by which we try to comprehend it.

Henri Wallon's researches in this field follow on the tradition of classical rationalism, that of Descartes, Spinoza, Leibniz, Kant, Fichte, Hegel and Marx, and not that of the minor positivist, scientist, dogmatic, and limited rationalism of the end of the nineteenth century.

Again, we would be mistaken if, pushing our inquiry into the roots of religion beyond its social roots, right back to those which derive from man's relations with nature, to those which derive from the very act of knowledge, we then attributed eternal life to religion. All we are showing, following Lenin, is that the religious attitude is not without foundation in knowledge itself. As he says, it is 'a barren flower, but a barren flower that has bloomed on the living tree of man's living knowledge.'

We cannot, therefore, avoid reflecting on the future of this 'great speculative adventure' of which Wallon writes, and seeing how what man has for countless centuries dreamed of in a religious form will develop in a non-mystified form, in an authentically scientific thought. Einstein has expressed with great clarity this problem of the relations between science and religion in our time. 'What,' he asks, 'are the feelings and needs that have led man to religious thought and belief in the widest sense of the words?' (*The World As I See It*, trans. Alan Harris, London, 1935, pp. 23-4).

After speaking of primitive man's fears as he confronts the forces of nature, and then dealing with the social roots of religion, he adds that beyond these anthropomorphic conceptions there is what he calls a 'cosmic religious feeling'. Man 'wants to experience the universe as a single significant whole' (p. 25). This 'cosmic religious feeling is the strongest and noblest incitement to scientific research'. It is 'a deep conviction of the rationality of the universe', a 'rapturous amazement at the harmony of natural law' (p. 28). And of this 'cosmic religious feeling which as yet acknowledges neither dogmas nor God,' he adds, 'it is the most important function of art and science to awaken it and keep it alive' (p. 26).

This is not to say that religion will never die: it means the determination to lose no part of the human riches that have been won through mankind's religious experience, and to develop all those dimensions of man which for so many thousand years have been explored in the mystified form of divine attributes.

*

What contribution, then, has Christianity, which has played so large a part in our area of civilisation, made to our concept of man?

The fundamental and constant characteristic of the ancient Graeco-Roman wisdom is that it situates and defines man in relation to a totality of which he is a phase or part, whether it be the cosmos or the city, the order of nature or the conceptual order.

From Thales to Democritus the world is conceived as a being that is *given*. Man can know it in its ultimate reality and through this *knowing* he can attain the highest dignity open to man: the consciousness of his own destiny, and happiness.

From Plato to the Stoics, it is again *knowing* which emancipates and leads to mastery of self and happiness, even if it is through different conceptions of ultimate reality, which can be sensible or intelligible, of the order of nature or of the conceptual order.

Standing at the watershed between these two great currents of ancient thought, Socrates, more than any other thinker, made *knowing*, which is the keystone of ancient humanism, the supreme end of man: the moment when, regaining possession of himself from his starting point in nature, he comes to realise that this rationality of the world is the very law of his own mind; the moment when the essential thing becomes precisely this consciousness of self, this discovery of meaning, that is, of the rational order.

This knowledge of self, if one taught, with Protagoras, that

man is the centre and measure of all things, might lead to individualism and a retreat into the isolated self; but with Socrates, in the dramatic presentation of the *Laws*, for example, it remains a profound awareness that the presence in man of reason is possible only because this man belongs to the city and this city dwells in him.

In this philosophy of *being*, man is greater the more he is *what is*, through his consciousness of this being, through his participation in this order, the order of the cosmos and of the city.

At first Christianity represents a break-away from this Hellenic concept of the world. As a continuation of Judaism, it substitutes a philosophy of *act* for a philosophy of *being*: in this philosophy of act, which is dominated not by the notion of 'logos' but by that of creation, man's value consists in having consciousness not indeed of what is, but *of what he is not*, of what he lacks.

With St Augustine, man is measured not in relation to the dimensions of the earth or the stars, nor according to the laws of the city or of any universal. He *exists*, not as part of a totality of nature or of concepts, but in his particularity, as subjectivity, as interiority, in virtue of the intervention of the God who dwells in him and removes him from every given 'order'. 'We overstep the narrow limits of our knowledge' writes St Augustine (*De Anima*, IV, 6, 8), 'we cannot take possession of ourselves, and yet we are not outside ourselves.'

In its violent reaction against pagan wisdom, primitive Christianity readily sacrificed, for this conquest of subjectivity and interiority, the rationality so patiently won by the aesthetic and rational humanism of Greek thought. In the fourth century, Lactantius (*Divinae Institutiones*, II, 5) argues for the will of God, against the fatalism of the Stoics and their concept of order and the rational.

The world is seen no longer as the inevitable unfolding of a rational law, but as a gift of love.

From this new conception of the world is derived a new conception of man: his goal is no longer the grandeur of being equated, by *knowledge*, with the eternal order of the cosmos and the sovereign law of the city. His infinite value is that he in turn is, in the image of God, creator with the capacity for gift and love, facing an absolute future which is not a logical extension of the past or a phase in a given totality, but the possibility of beginning a new life: to this he is called by a God who is no longer totality, nor concept, nor harmonious and completed image of the human order, but both a personal God and a hidden God, whom no knowledge can give us, and to whom only faith can open the road—always, however, in suffering and uncertainty.

Thus Graeco-Roman antiquity on the one hand, and Judaeo-Christian antiquity on the other, brought to light (but separately and in radical opposition to one another) two demands of humanism: the demand for a rational mastery of the world, and that for a specifically human historical initiative.

In the western tradition the problem and programme of humanism was henceforth to be the keeping hold of both ends of the chain even if we should be torn apart in so doing.

This the Renaissance did not succeed in doing: for at that time there appeared again with humanism—and once again separately—all the Graeco-Roman ambitions for a mastery, at once rational and mathematical, technical and experimental, of the world; and, with the Reformation, all the agonising Judaeo-Christian doubts, which derive from man's divine and infinite vocation and his own irreparable limitation, and came back with the theology of sin and grace in Luther and of predestination in Calvin.

The greatest minds stated the problem without finding a solution to it. Pico della Mirandola, in his *De Magnitudine Hominis*, gave paradoxical expression, in Christian terms, to the claim of Prometheus: 'We have given you, Adam, no form and no determined place in the world; but we have given you eyes with which to see it, and hands with which to mould it, so that it may depend on you alone whether you degrade yourself to the lower level of the brute beasts or raise yourself to the higher level of the divine beings.' In this wonderful promise of a great humanism we find side by side, but unconnected, the Greek sense of freedom, which is knowledge and power, and the Christian sense, which is gift, since for the Christian this freedom of knowledge and power is granted by God to man. The same unresolved dualism is still to be found in Descartes, forging the rational and mathematical tools which are to enable men to become masters and owners of nature, and at the same time asserting that even mathematical truths are such only by an arbitrary decree of God.

This uneasy equilibrium was to be upset immediately after Descartes and to give, on the one hand, in Leibniz's *Monadology*, the classic theory of the person—every soul is an image of the universe and every mind an image of God, 'every mind is a little divinity in its own sphere'—and on the other hand, over against this God-filled world, that of the eighteenth-century French materialists, a world empty of God and promising man, within a naturalist conception of necessity, absolute mastery of the universe, of society, and of himself.

The first attempt at the great synthesis came from the classical German philosophy, and notably from Kant and Fichte, who brought together the two ends of the chain in the concept of *autonomy*, the necessity of the rational law without which there is no science and no world, and the freedom of man's creative act, without which there is no moral initiative and responsibility and no history.

Once again, however, the chain broke, for the synthesis was never effected. Kant tried in vain to bring about the unity of reason and freedom of science and ethics, of pure reason and practical reason, in a theory of art which he himself realised rested on the postulate of an ultimate harmony. The ageing Fichte moved from a 'doctrine of science', based on a free act of reason, to a mysticism in which science and reason are ultimately subordinated to faith, and man's free creation to an assent to the will of God.

Goethe's Faustian equilibrium of knowledge and freedom still remained a dream and a promise, the finest of humanity's dreams and promises, but still a dream, always recurring and always postponed.

The divergence is found again in Hegel's majestic rational system of nature and history on the one hand, and on the other in Kierkegaard's insistence on both subjectivity, radical in its particularity, and transcendence.

Christianity in fact raised the problem of transcendence, and with it, moreover, that of subjectivity; indeed, even the way of approaching the problem of subjectivity is specific to Christianity. Transcendence is a dangerous word, for it is burdened with a weighty past history of confusions and mystifications. Traditionally, the notion implies belief in the beyond, in the 'supernatural', with all that those notions contain of irrationality, of the miraculous, of mystery, and ultimately, of deception.

Does this mean that when we look at this central aspect of the religious attitude, we must not ask ourselves to what need, to what question, to what experience, this faith in transcendence corresponds?

Under the appeal to transcendence lies this real experience, that while man belongs to nature he differs from things and animals and that, with his capacity continually to outstrip himself, he is never a completed being.

As Marx explains, when, with the appearance of specifically human labour—of labour, that is, which has as its law the end or project aimed at—man raises himself above all the other animal species and begins an historical development whose rhythm is incommensurable with that of biological evolution, then we come up against a qualitative leap, a true supersession, a transcendence (in the strictly etymological sense of the word) in relation to nature. Man is part of nature, but with man, through culture, a higher level of nature begins to emerge. This is the real human core of this notion of transcendence: transcendence is the alienated expression of the leap beyond nature effected in culture. That the very creature who crossed this threshold, man, should have been so astounded by what he did that he imagined another order of reality than that of nature, a super-nature, a beyond, filled with promises and threats, that is the typical reaction of alienation. To work out a concept of dialectical supersession that is not alienated, is therefore to show—and dialectical materialism enables us to do this—that this possibility of initiative and creation is not an attribute of God: it is, on the contrary, the specific attribute of man, and the attribute which distinguishes him from all the other animal species.

This concept of transcendence enables us to bring out another aspect of the Christian contribution: the sense of *subjectivity*. While for Greek humanism man is a fragment of the universe and a member of the city, Christianity, following Judaism, emphasised the possibility for man of beginning a new future; it stressed the element of *subjectivity* in man's life. Between action coming from the external world and man's action going out to meet the external world in order to deal with this threat, lies consciousness at its various levels: pain and effort, quest and dream, hope and love, danger and decision. That is what subjectivity means. Christianity has accumulated a rich store of experience on this plane, from St Augustine to Kierkegaard, from Pascal and Racine to Claudel, while elaborating, in its adoption of the neo-platonist themes of renunciation of the external world, the doctrines of fatalism and resignation.

With transcendence and subjectivity, love is one of Christianity's most undeniable contributions to the figure of man. When the Christian speaks of the transcendence of love, when he thinks of it and even lives it in an alienated way, that is, in terms of exteriority (as Marx showed in *The Holy Family*

in connection with 'Fleur de Marie'[1]) we have to find out
what need, or suffering, or hope, can have brought him to
this alienation. If we have not first mutilated man by ruling
out all subjectivity and all true interiority and so reducing
him to being nothing but a product of social structures, completely determined by them; if, instead, we have shown, with
Marx, that what is stifled and crushed by the structures of
capital is precisely a human reality constantly developing in
history but not created in its entirety by the structures of the
time, and so capable of being a protest against them—then
we shall be able to understand how this or that impotent
protest has led to the projection outside this world, into another world, into a hereafter, of a love which is this iron
world's 'other'. It is only right to remind, as Marx did in
Capital, those who have constructed this dream in all honesty
that those who talk most about charity and love of one's
neighbour, have more often than not used those fine words
as a hypocritical excuse for perpetuating a social system
whose law is the opposite of love: permanent violence against
the worker and the perversion, by the very law of the régime,
of all human feelings; we should point out, too, as Engels did
in *The Origin of the Family*, what conditions must be realised
for a just and sound relationship between, for example, men
and women: in other words, socialism.

Nevertheless this criticism, just and necessary though it is,
must not be exclusively destructive; it must lead to the recognition of the existence of a real problem. It is a fact that even
within feudal or capitalist social relations it has been possible
for exemplary instances of love—even if they have come up
against sometimes fatal obstacles—to emerge and develop, to
find forms of human relationships which, while deeply rooted

---

[1] A character in a story by Eugène Sue, a serial-writer immensely popular
in the 1830's and 1840's. 'We come across Marie surrounded by criminals,
a prostitute, a serf in a criminals' tavern. In this debasement she preserves
a human nobleness of soul and a human beauty . . . that win for her the
name of Fleur de Marie' (*The Holy Family*, p. 225).

in the physiological relations, relations of production, and political relations from which they are born, cannot entirely be reduced to them.

This love has found admirable forms of artistic expression, from courtly poetry to Tristan and Iseult, from St Teresa of Avila to Racine, from Marceline Desbordes-Valmore to Aragon's *Le Fou d'Elsa*, from Eluard to Claudel's *The Satin Slipper*.

Conversely, we have henceforth historic proof of what Marx and Engels foresaw in theory when they recognised the relative autonomy of superstructures: it is not enough for socialism to establish new social relations if it is automatically to produce new human relations. Forms of sensibility and conceptions of love that are still feudal or bourgeois in type can still continue to exist in a socialism régime: sometimes perverted, as in the old régimes, sometimes, too, retaining the same human beauty as that which characterised what were its finest expressions in those régimes. It is still difficult to make out the features of a new human physiognomy of love: quite apart from the underestimating of the relative autonomy of superstructures which led, in films or novels, to lovers' conversations about productivity, it is a fact confirmed by experience that in the most successful works, in Sholokov or in *La Ballade du Soldat*, it is difficult to see what, in the poems or on the stage, differentiates the finest sentiments from those expressed in the great romantic or epic works of the past. A Christian feels perfectly at home in them. Here again we meet a problem, a problem of theory, which we cannot evade.

If we turn aside from this aspect of living reality, if we confine ourselves to the just and necessary critical denunciation of what, in the very law of a class régime, prevents the full flowering of a completely human love, then the Christian (even if he considers our demonstration perfectly just) will continue to recognise that this régime (though he may well call it, more inexactly and metaphysically, 'this world') de-

grades love, and so he will dream of 'another world', a 'hereafter' in which this aspiration for love will be satisfied.

*

Moreover, the specifically Christian attitude to love cannot
be confused with a variant of Platonism which contrasts 'the
other world' or 'the hereafter' with this world, and calls on
us to cut ourselves off from this world, to turn our backs on
it and emigrate to the 'other' world, to the hereafter, to
God.

This dualism, idealism, disincarnation is, on the other
hand, characteristic of heresy, from Docetism to the Cathars;
while the essential Christian teaching, even if it has often
been host to the parasite of Hellenism or gnosticism, is based
on incarnation, and entails very different relations with
the other man, our 'neighbour'. It means treating every being, no matter who, as though he were Christ, as though he
were the living God, standing before us. The love of man is
one with the love of God. That, moreover, is why the mystics,
following a tradition that is as old as the Song of Songs, speak
of the love of God in images appropriate to human love: as
can be seen, in particular, in St Teresa of Avila.

It is important to stress this cardinal aspect of the Christian
heritage, because—so long as we distinguish the true contribution of Christianity from all that it can sometimes be con-
verted into by what Nietzsche called 'a Platonism for the
masses'—the new dimensions and significance given to love
by Christianity are the richest contribution it has made to
the continued creation of man by man. At the same time, it
is what can be most fully integrated in the Marxist concept
of man and the world.

To show that this is so, one has only to compare the
Christian conception of love with the loftiest definition of
love given by the great humanism of Greece: to compare
Plato's 'eros' with the Christian 'agape'.

The Platonic concept of love or eros, in the *Symposium* or

137

the *Phaedrus*, is characterised by a movement which raises us up towards the supreme Being and the supreme good, by detaching us from the terrestrial world. In an ascending dialectic which carries us from love of the beauty of the body to love of the beauty of the mind, and so to love of beauty 'in itself', love (eros) takes us outside this world, outside other men, outside time. It is a desire that can be satisfied by nothing in the real world, a desire that is incompatible with the daily world of men. The other being, accordingly, is loved not for what it is but for that which it evokes of another reality. In this love there is no 'neighbour'. The other being is no more than opportunity to rise up towards a reality that is incommensurable with it. Thus everyone loves the other only from a starting point in himself: or rather, what he loves is not another being but love itself.

Before the teaching of Christianity entertained the parasitic growth of Hellenism, of Platonism, of gnosticism, and long before the centuries-old adulterations ranging from the *Imitation of Christ* to certain forms of courtly love which it inspired, right up to the modern and still current versions of a hypocritical condemnation of the flesh or a contempt of the world that was simply a form of self-interest, what was most radically new in Christianity was quite the opposite: it was its transition, through the central experience of the Incarnation, of the God-man and the man-God, from the love of love to the love of the other. It was that, through incarnate love, it gave an absolute value to the other man and to the world. In the fundamental (that is, the Christo-centric) Christian tradition, to turn to God in no way implies turning away from the world, since the living God can be met in every being. This is what Cardinal Bellarmine in the sixteenth century called 'the ascent to God by the ladder of created beings', and what in the twentieth century Père Teilhard de Chardin calls 'transcending by passing through': in 'the evolution of chastity' he writes that 'it is by carrying the world with us that we advance into the embrace of God,' and teaches us 'to find in the faith of Christ a leaven for natural activity.'

To give a concrete picture of Christianity's new contribution in the matter of love, even for those who have ceased to be Christians, we can contrast, in our own day, Platonic love with that of two of the greatest contemporary poets, Claudel and Aragon.

What is most striking in Claudel's love is precisely the force with which *the reality of the other being* is asserted. In his fine book, *Le drame de Claudel*, Jacques Madaule writes that 'the communion of saints sums up the whole of Claudel's drama.' Now, the communion of saints is not expressed in the abstract idea that the life of every man has repercussions on that of all other men. Claudel's 'poetic art' is founded on this certain belief that every being, in its own singularity, has need of all the others: each individual being calls for its complement, and this complement is nothing less than the entire universe. This is the profound significance of love, of a love that is indistinguishably both human and divine. For woman constitutes for man, and man for woman, the necessary complement. Spirituality cannot develop fully except in the couple. 'What are you, my daughter,' says Anne Vercors to Violaine, 'but the full flowering of what is feminine in me?' (cf. *The Tidings Brought to Mary*, trans. L. M. Sill, London, 1916, p. 51).

In every being, love is a witness to the impossibility of living in isolation. In Claudel, no doubt, as in all religious tradition, what lies before man as his task is to be found behind him, as his origin. This vast human project, always growing greater and always held up, of constructing and realising the unity and plenitude of man, is then seen, by an inversion which in our eyes is alienation, as a return to a primordial unity, as though the end of love were the reconstruction of our lost Paradise.

But what is still true, apart from this mystification, is that love of the other as other, in his radical otherness, calls us to emerge from ourselves, to break through our own limits and transcend ourselves. It is through love that 'the drop of water feels that the whole ocean is ever crying out for it' (*Cent phrases pour un éventail*). Thus every being finds in another the key to its own self, finds its own meaning. That is to say the revelation of the part it can play in a vaster totality. Love is initiation into the passion of the universe.

> '*I was awaiting an answer, but in my soul and my body I*
> *received*
> *More than an answer, the drawing out of all my substance,*
> *As the secret locked in the heart of the planets, the true bond*
> *That links my being to a greater being.*'

It is thus that Violaine speaks, and this is the language of love, too, which always points beyond itself. Physical desire takes on a new meaning in man. Religious mystification begins with the belief that this meaning has already in some way been impressed upon nature by a God; whereas for us Marxists the meaning does not exist at the level of nature but comes in only with the emergence of man, from the moment when, with work and the anticipation of ends which defines it as specifically human, in relation to this end or project, everything takes on meaning, and value can be born. For us, specifically human love is man's creation, not a gift of God. It is, for us, a decision of man's, a human initiative and responsibility, and not 'the inexorable summons of the wondrous voice'.

Love belongs to the order not of *nature* but of *culture*: for a value cannot be given 'from outside', even though the giver be a God. Nature precedes meaning. Only a human initiative can give meaning to that which precedes meaning: nature. In man, love, even physical love, is a fact not of nature but of culture. The victory of love is no more written beforehand into a providential plan than is any other victory, and if we are to conquer we cannot be dispensed from fighting.

Otherwise—and this line of thought is particularly significant in Claudel's last writings—every mind enters into a direct dialogue with God, without passing through the other being, and human love is no more than a phase that is super-seded, as subjectivity was in Hegel's 'absolute knowledge'. Claudel's *Christophe Colomb* is *The Satin Slipper* without Dame Prouheze; his *Jeanne d'Arc* is still *The Satin Slipper*, this time without Rodrigue de Manacor, and *Tobie et Sarah* is no longer the human dialogue of love but the language of allegory called in to evoke a higher reality, separate from the real couple.

One of the most striking characteristics of Aragon's work is its power of integrating, in a materialist and dialectical point of view, what is deepest in Christian love. This alone would suffice to give his work an exemplary character. More-over, Aragon in no way disguises this attempt by atheism to recover the divine. In his *Entretiens* on *Le Fou d'Elsa* he returns to a theme to which he had already referred: 'Marx turned the dialectic of the idealist Hegel the right side up again, and I want to try to do more or less the same with mysticism.' He gives an example of this 'reversal'. 'One of the greatest Arabic mystics, Ibn Arabi, said, "In reality, a being loves nobody but his creator": should one not reverse this proposition and say: he who loves me, creates me? This is the mystic's proposition expressed the right way round . . . For me this means, without any doubt, that the principle by which I am created is to be found in the very object of my love. At all events, here we have mysticism, diverted from God to woman, and in it I find an explanation of what poetry is . . . In *Le Fou*, poetry appears as mysticism put back on its feet, that is to say, as the source from which mysticism derives its strength . . . mysticism has changed its meaning: it has become poetry.'

It would be easy to make a mistake here, and liken Ara-gon's position to Feuerbach's, who substitutes for 'God is love' the phrase 'love is God'.

Just as the 'reversal' of Hegel by Marx cannot be likened to the 'reversal' of Hegel by Feuerbach, so the inversion of

Christian mysticism in Aragon cannot be likened to Feuer-bach's inversion of Christian love. Just as Marx was not satis-fied to invert Hegel's system by saying 'matter' where Hegel said 'mind', so Aragon is not satisfied to say 'love of Elsa' where the mystics say 'love of God'.

The inversion affects not the *system* but the *method*.

Here again, the *meaning* of love is not already written into nature by a God: the *meaning* is a specifically human creation. Aragon is vividly conscious of this. In the trial of Elsa's mad-man, when the Mejnun says of Elsa, 'I have given you the place reserved for God', and the judges raise a cry of sacrilege because in so doing he 'is offering an obscene worship to a woman who is visible', 'My son,' says the old man, 'how could man be sacrilegious when the whole law resides in him alone?'

Here we see the radical difference between Aragon's atheism and the Christian concept, even in the secularised but still 'naturalist' form given to it by Feuerbach.

Bearing that in mind, it still remains true that it is to Christian love that love owes, in Aragon, its being rooted in so great a depth of being.

In this connection, the poem to St John of the Cross, in *Le Fou d'Elsa*, is illuminating.

'*John of the Cross, I ask you*
What is man, and what is love . . .
John of the Cross, you are but the name the Christian gives to
all who in their love write their own doom.'

Surrealism saw in love the metaphysical experience of the marvellous, the most intimate form of man's relations with the world. For Aragon, it was the first stage of the 'reversal', corresponding to the Feuerbachian stage of Marx's reversal of Hegel.

Aragon's encounter with Marxism enabled him to go be-yond this phase, integrating it with a loftier conception.

Since *Les Cloches de Bâle*, love acquires an historical and social dimension. Just as Marx defined the individual as the sum of his social relations, so all the contradictions and all the lacerations of an age and a society are condensed in the pair of lovers, as though in a microcosm. That is why, in this torn-asunder world, 'there is no such thing as happy love'. In the fate of each couple, Bérénice and Aurélien, Cécile and Jean, Louis and Elsa, the whole fate of our century is reflected, is concentrated and bonded into one.

At the same time, however, love displays the specifically human dimension of history: poetry and love disclose man's transcendence in relation to each of his provisional realisations. This transcendence is the only transcendence known to atheists: the future. In this profound sense, 'woman is man's future'. With love, a new dimension is added to the world: Elsa's love is the promise and warrant of a fully human future.

In virtue of Bérénice's experience, who dares to 'pursue in this being of flesh the quest for the absolute,' Aragon tells us, 'there is but one passion so devouring that no words can describe it . . . it is the hunger for the absolute.'

Thereby all idolatry is transcended: 'From the God who is negated, a new God is born.' All opposition, too, between master and slave, being and having: 'Love is a place in which is developed this knowledge which is never possession.' 'Poetry is the being which carries knowledge beyond having.'

Swept along in such a movement towards the other in his particularity which insists that we detach ourselves from impersonal totality, Aragon can thus exclaim:

'Listen to me, you people of Christ, we too have loved.'

Love is a privileged experience of the profound truth that the genesis of mind takes place through and not outside matter, that mind is not the opposite of nature but the information of nature.

Just as the moral value of actions is in proportion to the energy with which they inspire us, so the quality of a love is judged by the richness of the thoughts and actions it stimulates in us, by the dormant energies it arouses.

It may well be that through love we grasp being itself in its working, in its creative future, and that we can see it in that force which Père Teilhard had in mind when he wrote, 'Some day, after harnessing the winds, and the tides, and gravity, we shall harness, for God, the energies of love. And then, for the second time in the history of the world, man will have discovered fire.'

*

Doubts are sometimes cast on the possibility of Marxism's integrating in its concept of the world and of man, the essential element in Christianity's contribution to the figure of man. This leads, for example, to contesting the ability of Marxism to provide a theoretical basis for the recognition of the absolute value of the human person.

Two recent studies, by Christian writers who at the same time have an excellent knowledge of Marxist philosophy and a particular understanding of communism, provide evidence of this difficulty. These are Pastor Gollwitzer's *Athéisme marxiste et foi chrétienne* and Fr. Girardi's studies on *Umanesimo marxista ed umanesimo cristiano*.

The fundamental objections raised by these two writers may be reduced to three.

1. Pastor Gollwitzer writes: 'In Marx the human species is substituted for the absolute spirit of Hegel. In both cases, in Marx as in Hegel, if the individual has no meaning or reality except in relation to the totality which gives them to him, then the realisation of the individual means his total absorption in the process of realisation of the species. The right of the species destroys the right of the man as person.'

2. Fr. Girardi starts by offering a variation of the above objection. He says: for Marxism, the absolute is not man but humanity. By this subordination to this higher end, man has no value other than that which he receives from his end.

3. Fr. Girardi more or less sums up all these objections

in a single one: the Marxist conception of praxis and revolution as absolute value and as the criterion of value does not appear to be reconcilable with the principle of the absolute value of the person.

These objections are based on a conception of Marxism which confuses it either with Hegelianism or with pragmatism; underlying them, is a threefold confusion.

1. *The erroneous assimilation of Hegel's absolute spirit and the human species in Marx.* Marx, we have seen, was not content to reverse Hegel's system by saying *matter* where Hegel says *spirit.* It was Hegel's *method* he reversed (a different problem with which we are not here concerned), and he did not reverse but entirely rejected Hegel's *system* and even the Hegelian concept of it. Marx postulates neither absolute knowledge nor an end to history. Therein lies the whole, and capital, difference between a *closed* system and an *open* method of endless creation.

Marx does not conceive a closed totality which assigns to each of its parts its own place. (That was later to be the totalitarian, fascist, and even racialist interpretation of the human species or the nation, in which the individual has no significance and reality except by virtue of the whole to which he belongs.) What Marx did conceive was a continued creation of man by man. Communism is not the end of history but the end of man's brutish pre-history, and the beginning of a strictly human history, made up of all the initiatives of each human person, now become the centre of creation in all domains, from economic life to culture. In the *Communist Manifesto* Marx defined communism as 'an association in which the free development of each is the condition for the free development of all.'

2. *Confusion between the pragmatic conception and the Marxist conception of the criterion of practice.*

For a Marxist, the practice which is ultimately the criterion of truth is not an individual or individualist practice. It is the practice of the collective body to which man belongs, with all the culture which that society brings with it. But it has above all an historical character. Thus its effectiveness is not defined simply by the immediate result and the profitability of an action which at every moment is an absolute beginning. The act and its value are judged first in terms of a human history whose meaning is not patient of arbitrary revision at every moment. From man's simplest project by which he releases himself, through the tool, from the immediate given situation, to the power to transform the planet by a concerted use of nuclear energy, human societies have created their history; and it is possible to determine the position of each stage and evaluate it in terms not of a final goal but of the degree of mastery over nature, over society and over himself, that man has won. Ultimately, the criterion of practice cannot be defined if we leave out of account this ascending curve of the conquest of a real freedom. This rules out all forms of pragmatism, from that of the individualist thruster to that of the political adventurer, placing the mystification of the masses on the same level as their awakening to consciousness of the laws of historical development. For a Marxist, the criterion of practice cannot be reduced to the criterion of immediate success, whether it be individual or collective. It is a function of the realisation of the fundamental human project, that which starts from the definition of man as creator and aims to make of every man a creator.

3. This, again, gets rid of the third confusion on which these objections are based: *the confusion of the end and the means*.

For a Marxist, the social revolution is not an end in itself nor an ultimate end. The ultimate end of all our actions and all our battles as militant communists is to make *every* man a man, that is to say a creator, a centre of historical initiative and of creation on the economic and political plane, on the plane, too, of culture and love, on the spiritual plane—to use an idiom that is not ours. (That idiom, however, is not ours precisely because people too often when speaking of the spiritual disregard the material conditions that are necessary for the free development of spirituality.) It is true enough that while the social revolution—that is, the abolition of the régime based on private ownership of the means of production—is not the ultimate end and the criterion of all value, it is at the same time an absolutely essential means for the free development of the person; and all sermonising about spirituality that neglects this prime condition of its realisation, and all theorising about ends that has nothing to say about means, is a deception: it is an hypocritical alibi which exalts the human person while helping to perpetuate the historical conditions of its degradation.

What then, from a Marxist point of view, is the theoretical basis of the absolute value of the human person?

The misunderstanding with the Christian interpreters of Marxism originates in Marx's sentence: 'A being does not regard himself as independent unless he is his own master, and he is only his own master when he owes his existence to himself' (*Manuscripts of 1844*, in *Early Writings*, p. 165).

This, according to Pastor Gollwitzer, is an impoverishing conception of man and of freedom, since it cuts man off both from the world of things and from that of men, and abandons us to bare solitude.

This objection is based on a mistaken reading of Marx.

Such a definition of freedom cannot be interpreted in the sense that would be attributed to it either by the idealist Hegel or by the individualist Stirner.

Unlike Hegel, Marx, being a materialist, does not hold that the world of things is the product of our own mind.

Marx, therefore, does not postulate a subject who creates the world, in the Hegelian way, nor a subject who maintains the relations with the object which were conceived by Cartesian dualism. Marx, on the contrary, emphasises the constant reciprocal action between man and the beings found in nature, external to him and independent of him.

An objective being, he says, is a being which has its nature 'outside itself'. It creates, it postulates objects, only because it is itself postulated by objects, because in its origin it is nature.

Hunger, for example, ties it to an object outside itself which can satisfy that need.

Thus no natural being can exist nor be conceived outside the network of reciprocal actions upon which it depends and which, to some degree, depend upon that being.

When Marx speaks of man's autonomy and independence we should not, therefore, understand them in the sense they were understood by the idealist Hegel, for whom the isolated subject constructed its object in its entirety.

Marx does not confuse *objectivation* and *alienation*: the external world is not for him a simple alienation of the subject, nor a radical creation of the object by the subject.

For Marx, the materialist, the subject endeavours actively —that is, by a series of hypotheses, theories, models—to reconstruct this world of objects which exists without him and does not need him in order to exist.

The resistances offered by reality to the subject's models— continually more complex though they are—are, as Lenin showed, an 'inexhaustible' source of enrichment, and it is this alone that makes it possible to account for the history of knowledge, which, from the idealist point of view, is always a false and apparent history.

This is even more true when we are concerned not only with other things but with other men.

Unlike the individualist Stirner, Marx defines the individual (in the theses on Feuerbach) by the 'sum of his social relations'.

There could be no greater mistake than to interpret this sentence in a mechanistic sense: the individual is not a mere product or resultant.

No greater mistake, again, than to believe that man does not exist for Marxism, that what does exist is a sum of social relations; that men are not the subject of history but only the effects and the props of a sum of social relations; that in Marx there is no centre, no subjects who create meaning, no men who make history—an idea that has for a long time been disseminated by the opponents of Marxism and has to-day been brought up again in a new form, based on a certain interpretation of structural linguistics and Freudism, by ideologists who claim to follow the Marxist tradition.

Marx explicitly rules out this interpretation: he emphasises on the contrary the contradiction, characteristic of every class régime, between the personal life of man and the economic and social system which tends to make of him a mere support for production relationships.

In *The German Ideology*, he stresses 'the contradiction between the personality of the individual proletarian and the conditions of life which are imposed on him' (p. 288). 'In the course of historical development,' he adds, 'with division of labour a distinction becomes apparent between the life of every individual as a personal life and as being subordinated to a particular branch of labour.' Marx was never to vary his views on this point, and what he has to say about it in *Capital* is as explicit as it is in *The German Ideology*.

It is precisely this that distinguishes Marxism from earlier materialism, which led to a misunderstanding of subjectivity which amounted to seeing in it nothing but a passive reflection of an external world, presented ready-made in its mechanistic structure. In the third of the theses on Feuerbach, Marx already stresses this distinction. 'The materialist doctrine that men are products of circumstances and upbringing and that, therefore, changed men are products of other circumstances, forgets that *it is men who change the circumstances*' (in *The German Ideology*, pp. 665-6).

On this point, again, Marx was never to vary; he constantly recalls, from *The Eighteenth Brumaire of Louis Bonaparte* to *Capital*, that it is men who make history. 'It is man, the real, living man, who is the maker, the possessor, the fighter. It is not history that uses man to become real: history is simply the activity of man pursuing his end' (cf. *The Holy Family*, trans. R. Dixon, London, 1957, p. 125).

This shows how wrong it would be to interpret in a mechanistic or positivist sense the phrase that Engels borrowed from Hegel, 'Freedom is the recognition of the inevitable.'

This should be understood in the light of another of Marx's definitions: 'Freedom is the consciousness man has of himself in the element which is at work in practice. In other words it is the knowledge man has of another man as his equal' (cf. *Ibid*).

Here we reach the heart of the problem, the problem of freedom, of Marxist humanism; it is the problem both of subjectivity and of man's relations with another man and with the world.

For man, the driving force of history is not the abstract subject, the spirit of Hegel.

Nor is this man, the driving force of history, the self-centred and isolated individual extolled by the anarchist Stirner. After having written 'Freedom=power' in *The Holy Family*, Marx adds, in *The German Ideology*: 'It is in the community that the individual acquires the means of developing his faculties in every direction: it is only in the community that freedom of the person becomes possible.'

What, then, is the human person for Marx, if it is neither Hegel's abstract subject nor Stirner's isolated individual?

For Marx, the individual is defined by the sum of his social relations, just as the object is defined by its relations with the sum total of other objects, continuing inexhaustibly into infinity.

The reality with which the physicist deals, coming to grips with inanimate matter, is already (as Lenin said) 'inexhaustible'. How much more inexhaustible, then, is this matter which has crossed countless other thresholds of complexity, with its transition into life, into consciousness, and society.

Let us simply combine the thesis that matter, at all its levels, is inexhaustible, and the thesis that with work there emerged a radically new form of material being, in which the future, through the end pursued and the project, plays an active part and creates possibilities up to infinity. Let us add to this that these nuclei of being, of which each one thinks and creates, and which react upon one another, do not exist fully except in mutual exchange and dialogue, and so endlessly enrich one another; we shall then understand the richness of the Marxist concept of humanity, and appreciate the basis of its recognition of each man as an active and creative being.

It is wrong, therefore, to assimilate Marxism with some sort of Messianic belief, and then to say that it undermines the foundations of its own humanism, on the ground that it cannot justify the respect due to each human person because the only meaning it gives to each man's life is that it serves to realise the ends of the species. It is wrong to say that Marxism evades this problem and that to attach the function of the individual life to the service of the species is a contradiction of the humanist spirit. It is only a positivist distortion or a mechanistic interpretation of Marxism that is open to such a criticism; and I recognise, indeed, that too many such 'anti-humanist' distortions and interpretations have been found and can still be found in writings that claim to represent Marxism.

Conversely, however, the just concern to look at men one by one as individuals, with respect for their person and its absolute value, cannot paralyse our efforts to win a more human organisation of social relations.

This is a battle that must be fought, and the problem of means is exactly the same for Christians as it is for Marxists. Christians cannot evade it: we are never free to choose between violence and non-violence. We are already committed, and our abstention, equally with our engagement, plays its part in this confrontation of forces. To condemn the violence of the slave who revolts, is to become an accessory to the permanent violence of the enslaver. And that is why, if

Christians accept military service (and this they have never refused since the time of Constantine), why should they not fight for the Resistance or as military revolutionaries? If they refuse to do so, it is not the *means* they refuse—since, as soldiers, they accept violence—it is the revolutionary *end* itself.

History has taught Marxists to distrust the specifically religious component in anti-communism. It derives from the confusion of ethics with logic and from the claim to be able to deduce forms of political or social order directly from faith, without recognising the autonomy of the secular world and the fact that the mediations of purely scientific knowledge are indispensable for a judgment on a system of social relations or a political régime.

What a communist hates in the religious institution is what makes it hand in glove with the counter-revolution. He cannot be certain that the Church rejects communism primarily because it is atheistic. He suspects that it is much more because it is revolutionary. No true dialogue can be established until being a Christian does not necessarily mean being a defender of the established order.

As soon as Christians cease to reject *all* violence—by accepting military service and engaging in war—then to refuse to share in the violence that is essential to the battle that is fought in the name of respect for the human person, for the liberation of man, comes uncommonly close, in fact, to making that respect an excuse for, and a factual participation in, the hidden violence that maintains the existing order and oppression. The dialectical tension between the individual and the totality, between the end and the means, which is the tragedy of all action, is just as real for the Christian as it is for the Marxist. To contrast Christianity as it should be with communism as it is, is a false evasion of this tension. It is the same with the tension between the present and the future. It is not a question of sacrificing a whole contemporary generation to some vague future Utopia, which will turn out to be a Moloch. What gives meaning and beauty and value to life, for Marxists as for Christians, is the unstinting gift of self to what the world, through our sacrifice, can become in the future.

Pastor Gollwitzer distorts the terms of the problem when he repeats Koestler's question: 'What consolation can the unclouded happiness of future generations of sheep be to the sheep driven to the slaughter house?'

Nevertheless, there are fine things in his book, and one cannot but read with emotion—since a Marxist can recognise in them a tone of real fraternity—the pages in which he comments on the text from the Epistle to the Romans (8.24): 'For in this hope we were saved.' Rejecting a debased Christian Platonism, he shows that this should not be interpreted in a sense which postpones man's fulfilment to another world, but rather in the sense that this hope transfigures our life here and now.

As a Marxist, I would add: provided that this hope is only the interior side of a real fight, of a militant and combatant life, in a man who is conscious of containing within himself the future in embryo.

It is not by chance that in our own time communism, which makes revolutionaries not for revenge but in order to obtain fullness of life, has produced the greatest number of witnesses, for whom the Greek word is 'martyrs'.

It is in those martyrs that we find this presence of the future in embryo, which gives meaning and beauty to a life and death, and with it the feeling that this future is not an abstract idea, but the lived presence of all other men, each with his irreplacable unique personality, and with the power to add to each other man his inexhaustible richness: it can be seen in every line of the letters written by those who faced the firing squad, in the letters of Lacazette or Péri, in that of the young Greek communist Yannis Tsitsilonis, who was shot at the age of twenty, writing lovingly to his mother, 'When the day of freedom comes, when the bells ring out their message of joy and victory, you will say to yourself, that it is your son Yannis who is ringing them.'

It is not a matter of sacrificing the freedom of each man, his life and its meaning, to the Moloch of an abstract future, but, in Eluard's words, of 'moving from one man's horizon to the horizon of all men.'

It is not right to say, as Pastor Gollwitzer does, that Marxism cannot understand 'the relation between religion and the problem of the meaning of existence' (p. 145), and that, for the Marxist, that problem is shelved in favour of the positivist scheme which sees the individual and the future society of communism standing in the relation of means to end.

The living, concrete, community of other men, of which each man, let me repeat, is an inexhaustible centre of richness and interrogation for each other centre, is so profoundly the fundamental reality that, in the Marxist humanist point of view, each individual—or rather each person—can develop freely and fully only if he is immersed in that community and so draws from it warmth and life. But at no time can we forget that in every class régime the effect of relationships of exploitation and oppression, with all the forms of alienation they produce, is precisely to nullify this human communication. Our first objective, as militants, is the battle against those obstacles. As Marx wrote, 'The real, active orientation of man to himself as a species-being . . . is only possible in so far as he really brings forth all his species-powers, which is only possible through the co-operative endeavours of mankind and as an outcome of history' (*Manuscripts of 1844* in *Early Writings*, pp. 202-3).

In a communist régime, 'the question of the meaning of existence will still be raised, and there will still be depths to be sounded in the heart of man.'

This, however, also means that we must fight against everything which, in our class régimes, impoverishes and mutilates man by alienating him. And we shall never win that battle unless the fighting is shared by all who have the future at heart.

*

If we do not want to end up with a mechanical confrontation of two closed futures, we must somehow realise, both Christians and Marxists, that we cannot have mutual knowledge of one another without both becoming different.

This presupposes in the first place that we must not regard ourselves as possessing a truth given once and for all, definitive and ready-made.

It is of the very nature of Marxism to think of itself in this way, in historical terms. Engels emphasised that materialism would necessarily have to assume a new form with every epoch-making discovery in scientific history. On countless occasions Lenin recalled the necessity of this constant re-fashioning. 'We by no means take Marx's teaching as something complete and untouchable. On the contrary, we believe that all it has done is to lay the corner stones of the science which socialists must push forward in every direction if they are not to lag behind life' (*Works*, Vol. IV, pp. 217-18).

Every attempt to imprison Marxism in a closed system of principles or laws is contrary to its very essence.

Contemporary theology, too, seems to be moving towards the idea that the original conceptualisation of the faith in the forms of Greek thought is no more than one of its possible cultural forms.

The same massive facts of our century as oblige us to think Marxism in the spirit of our time, have led Christians to reflect deeply on the significance of their faith and the historic forms of its expression.

1. *The building of socialism on a global scale*, a major reality of our time, raises completely new problems both for Christians and for Marxists.

For every Christian who can distinguish, in the building of socialism, what derives from the actual principles of

Marxism, and what is the result of the historical conditions peculiar to each country, this building raises problems which are such as to make it possible to dissociate the Christian faith from social or political doctrines which bear the stamp of an age that is past.

(a) In the first place the possibility has been proved of new social relations which are not founded on a hierarchy of classes, sanctioned by the Church as being a consequence of sin.

(b) Secondly, the experience of new forms of social ownership makes it possible to re-think, in a new historical perspective, the postulate that private property, including private ownership of the means of production, constitutes a guarantee of the freedom of the human person. Millions of Christians now think along these lines, and their ideas came out into the open at the Vatican Council; and although the problem has not been solved, it has at least been raised.

2. *The movement of national liberation* for peoples who have been for many years colonialised, and their attainment of independence, have disclosed sources of values other than those of a civilisation known as 'western and Christian' and for long regarded as a model.

This vast movement of decolonisation has obliged Christians to revise their idea of the Church's 'missionary' function. All the problems have asserted themselves simultaneously: the political problem of the dangerous alliance of the missionary and the colonialist, the moral problems of the paternalist concept of missions, and finally the theoretical problem of the recognition of forms of spirituality and of values which do not originate in Christianity. In the case of the religions of Asia and Africa, and of Islam, it is not only the crusading spirit that is challenged but the very spirit of conversion.

The Council's decisions on freedom of religious belief, on the recognition of the non-Christian and secular world as a world to be reckoned with, of pluralism, and of the necessity of dialogue, mark a decisive step in this conscious realisation.

3. Finally, the *acceleration,* unprecedented in history, *of the rhythm of scientific and technical development,* and the very form it is taking, now no longer merely cumulative and quantitative but effected by a series of global reorganisations of the whole of the conceptual field, is bringing about a fundamental re-thinking of our concepts of the world in a humanist and critical outlook.

For Christians, this is expressed in an effort made by those of them who see things most clearly, to dissociate what is fundamental in their faith from the obsolete conceptions of the world in which that faith is traditionally expressed.

This movement can be seen in the attempt at demytholo-gising for which, as early as 1941, the Protestant theologian Bultmann called, in his contribution to a book (*Kerygma and Myth*) which inaugurated a new era of religious thought. Pastor Dietrich Bonhoeffer's admirable *Letters and Papers from Prison* follows the same line and is itself also a sign of the times.

In a more general way the problem is that of the relation-ship of science and faith, a problem that arises today in a form not met with before, through the recognition of the radical autonomy of scientific thought, which means that we must no longer try to fit faith into the misconceptions, con-stantly open to revision, of knowledge.

This change of attitude towards science entails a reversal of attitude towards the secular world as a whole, considered as autonomous and of major importance.

It is becoming progressively more difficult not to accept the distinction between *religion* as ideology and conception of the world, as the cultural form assumed by faith at a particular period of historical development, and *faith* itself.

This has already been stressed: a Protestant philosopher, Paul Ricoeur, can say today, 'Religion is the alienation of faith' (*De l'interprétation,* p. 159). Defining the 'horizon' as the 'metaphor of what comes closer without ever becoming an object of possession' (*Ibid,* p. 505), he believes that 'the idol is the reification of the horizon into thing.'

The same problem of the distinction between faith and the historical, provisional, cultural forms into which it has settled down, is forcibly raised by a Catholic philosopher, Leslie Dewart, who restates, at a new historical stage, Père Laberthonnière's theses on 'Christian realism and Greek idealism.'

Leslie Dewart recalls in the first place that the condition for the universalising or catholicising of Christianity, from St Paul to St Augustine, was its Hellenisation. The new conception of man's relations with the world which was born with Christianity from a starting point in Judaism, flowed into a pre-existing cultural form; that of Greek thought, which introduced into Christianity its own ideal perfection, stability. Hellenisation thus led to the petrification of dogma. Centuries later, the rediscovery of Aristotle reinforced still further this tendency, with medieval scholasticism, in whose idiom the Christian faith has, for the most part, been expressed until our own times.

The Christian concept of God has always been more or less contaminated by Parmenides' concept of being, by Plato's Idea of the Good, by Aristotle's first cause and prime mover, or the One of Plotinus.

To take but one example: all the attempts of theologians and Christian philosophers, decade after decade, to refurbish the 'proofs of the existence of God', have failed to detach the 'ontological argument' from its origins. The very way in which the problem is expressed derives entirely from the postulate of Parmenides, asserting the identity of being and intelligibility. The scholastics were satisfied to distinguish, in creatures, essence and existence, but at the same time held that in God the two were identified.

Removed from this typically Greek form of expressing the problem, the ontological argument is meaningless.

This expression of the problem, however, no longer corresponds to anything in living contemporary thought.

Hence, side by side with the attempts to construct a non-Cartesian theory of knowledge, a non-Platonic ethic, and a non-Aristotelian aesthetic, we have the attempt, constantly renewed in the twentieth century, to think in terms of a non-Hellenic theology.

Maurice Blondel, at least in the first version of *Action*, was perhaps the first pioneer of this new apologetics; but the most general tendency to escape from the Greek conception of the relationship between being and intelligibility was expressed in the attempts to theologise the philosophies of existence: the resurrection of Kierkegaard, and the flowering of 'dialectical theology' that started with Karl Barth, the theological variants of Jaspers and Heidegger, Bultmann and Fr. Karl Rahner, are evidence of this effort.

However, this was not in itself sufficient to lay the ghost of the Greek concept of being, which, by contaminating the Christian concept of God, caused the threat of the docetist heresy to become endemic in Christian thought, with its emphasis on the divinity of Christ at the expense of his humanity.

The root of the problem is that Greek philosophy offers no way of expressing what is the very heart of Christianity, the Incarnation.

The most Greek thought succeeded in doing, with Aristotle, was to conceive the transition from potency to act, while what our age needs above all is a philosophy based on creative development.

It is this, no doubt, that accounts for the impact of Père Teilhard de Chardin on so many Christian minds. It is sometimes said that Père Teilhard was not a theologian. I am no judge of that. Others say that his scientific works, and still more his extrapolations, are open to criticism. That may well be so. Others again say that what he offers is not a philosophy. This I can believe, because in our time there can be no pre-critical philosophy and still less any philosophy of nature.

None of this can alter the fact that Teilhard de Chardin presented his Church, and, even further, all men of our own time, with a fundamental problem—the fundamental problem of our century, the very problem which Marx raised for the first time a hundred years ago, and for the solution to which he provided the first elements: how are we to think of what is emerging for the future and control it?

This discovery by Marx is at the root of the most profound transformation of the world known to history. The question raised by Père Teilhard for Christians demanded from them nothing short of a reversal of their attitude to the world. He recalled a fundamental aspect of Christianity which has often been obscured by a latent Platonism, that to progress towards God does not mean that one must turn one's back on the world: on the contrary, each man shares fully in his own transformation and construction, with all that is clearest in his thought, most urgent in his action, and most powerful in his passion.

From such a point of view God is no longer a being nor even the totality of being, since no such totality exists and being lies entirely open to the future which has to be created.

Faith, then, is not the possession of an object by knowledge. St John of the Cross was already saying that faith does not meet an object, it meets 'nothing'. He spoke of the 'experience of the absence of God' and added in his *Ascent of Mount Carmel*: 'It is by this that one can recognise whether someone truly loves God, or whether he is satisfied with something less than God' (cf. *Works*, trans. E. Allison Peers, London, 1934, Vol. I, p. 373). God's transcendence implies his constant negation, since God is beyond all essence and all existence; he is constant creation.

A faith that was no more than an affirmation would be mere credulity.

Doubt is an integral part of living faith.

The depth of a believer's faith depends on how strong is the atheist in him—for it is that which protects him from all idolatry. 'They call us atheists,' wrote Justin. 'Indeed, we admit it, we are the atheists of these self-styled Gods' (I *Apology*, 6.1).

Pastor Dietrich Bonhoeffer was undoubtedly, in the middle of the twentieth century, one of the pioneers of this return to fundamentals. Christian theology, he thought, has always been a form of religion, a form of man's expression, which is a function of history; and he asked this question: 'If religion is no more than the garment of Christianity—and even that garment has had very different aspects at different periods—then what is a *religionless* Christianity?' (*Letters and Papers from Prison*, Fontana edn., p. 91).

Following what is nevertheless a very different road from Teilhard's, Bonhoeffer coincides with Teilhard's central experience: 'Religious people speak of God when human perception is (just from laziness) at an end, or human resources fail . . . always, that is to say, helping out human weakness or as a support in human failure . . . I should like to speak of God not on the borders of life but at its centre, not in weakness but in strength, not, therefore, in man's suffering and death but in his life and prosperity' (p. 93).

'The fundamental principle of the Middle Ages is heteronomy in the form of clericalism . . .' (p. 121) but 'it calls for a great evolution to lead the world to its autonomy.'

'This is the decisive difference between Christianity and all other religions. Man's religiosity makes him look in his distress to the power of God in the world . . . The Bible, however, directs him to the powerlessness and suffering of God . . . To this extent we may say that the process we have described by which the world came of age was an abandonment of a false conception of God, and a clearing of the decks for the God of the Bible, who conquers power and space in the world by his weakness. This must be the starting point for our "worldly" interpretation' (p. 122).

Bonhoeffer also says, 'I am giving much thought to the outward aspect of this religionless Christianity . . . It may be that on us in particular, midway between East and West, there will fall an important responsibility' (p. 93).

Here the dialogue is set at the highest level, that of the

integration, by each one, of the negation contained in the other as such.

For, just as we said that, for the believer, the depth of his faith depends on the strength of the atheist in him, so too, we may say that, for the atheist, the depth of his humanity depends on the strength of the believer in him.

In the development of this essential dialogue, as Lombardo-Radice has said, 'Co-existence does not mean living side by side, but growing together,' and in that dialogue the greatest tragedy that could occur would be for the class positions adopted by the hierarchy of the Church to make it impossible for the masses who are fighting for freedom from exploitation and oppression, to appreciate the richness and beauty of the Christian message.

When the encyclical *Quadragesimo anno* (1931) says that 'the capitalist system is not intrinsically evil', and when a few years later (1937) *Divini Redemptoris* insists that 'communism is intrinsically a perversion', is this said in the name of theology and the faith, or is it a political and class option?

Recent statements from the most authoritative sources in the Church in France and the universal Church, confirm the Church's attitude in allying itself with the privileged classes and their power, and giving its moral and doctrinal sanction to the privileged state and régime. This attitude was first adopted in the fourth century in the Church's relations with the Emperor Constantine, and in 1966 this Constantinianism is still by no means dead.

The least mistakes of communists are forcefully denounced.

The worst crimes of the capitalist world from Spain to Portugal, from Los Angeles to Vietnam, are passed over in silence.

The Church that really deserves the name of 'the Church of silence' is the Church that is silent in the face of crime.

One great hope remains, common to millions of Christians in the world and millions of communists: the building up of the future without losing anything of the heritage of human values that Christianity has been contributing for the last two thousand years. And yet we see this message obscured by class positions which hide and contradict the values contained for us in Christianity.

So long as this is so, there will be a great danger that once again, because of this class solidarity, the political and social liberation of man will be effected in opposition to Christianity. To rebut the charge of being 'the opium of the people', in which Marx and later Lenin summed up an irrefutable historical experience, is more than a matter of theory: it is a matter of political and social practice. And it is for Christians and their Church to give this practical proof.

If this is not done, then irreplaceable human values will be for a time compromised, and we shall be faced by the dreadful but unavoidable choice which Jaurès expressed in sombre and exalted words: 'Even if the socialists extinguish for a moment all the stars in the heavens, I am ready to march with them along the dim road that leads to justice, the divine spark which has the power to rekindle all the suns in all the furthest depths of space.' Here, perhaps, we have one of the most acute problems of our century. Shall we be forced to make this choice? Speaking as brother to brother, but with all the force that comes from our agony of anxiety, we warn Christians and their Church that it would be so much time lost for mankind.

CHAPTER FIVE

Marxism and Art

*

It is from the creative act of man, we have said, that Marxism starts.

It is there, too, that it ends up: making of each man a man, that is a creator, a 'poet'.

Where, then, does artistic creation stand in the development of the human act of labour, of the continued creation of man by man?

How can myth be a component of action to transform the world?

We have already emphasised that in passing from Utopia to science, socialism has not destroyed the dream. All it has done is to provide a scientific and technical basis for its realisation.

'We must dream,' said Lenin, who knew that myth is life in action.

From this humanist point of view, myth lies at the level of man's creative art, neither above nor below.

Just as we do not believe, with Berkeley, that nature is the symbolic language spoken by an infinite mind to finite minds, so we do not believe, with Cassirer, that myth is the Odyssey of the consciousness of God, with Gusdorf that it is immersion and metaphysical reintegration in reality, or with Duméry that it is a 'sensing' of pre-existing values; nor, again, do we think, with Jung, that the 'archetype' or 'primordial image' is the matrix of the idea. Myth is not a foothold in the sacred, nor in an initial nature.

If it speaks the language of transcendence, this transcendence cannot be thought of in terms of exteriority or presence. It is neither the transcendence from above of a God, nor the transcendence from below of a nature given to us ready-made.

Myth is not participation but creation.

Myth, for Marx, is not, as it is for Freud, even a sublimated expression of *desire*, but a phase of *labour*.

The difference is fundamental, for *desire* is a continuation of nature, whereas *labour* transcends it.

To make labour the matrix of myth—as, moreover, of all *culture* as opposed to *nature*—allows us already to draw the dividing line between the dream-symbol and the myth-symbol. The former is the expression of desire, the latter is a phase of the continued creation of man by man, in a form that is poetic, prophetic and militant, but always forward-looking.

This removes the confusion between myth properly so-called and what is wrongly given that name. If myth is the phase of labour in which the emergence of man asserts itself with the new dimension of being *what realises the future*, then we cannot give the name of myth to what is a mere survival of the past, the indolent and superseded reason of allegory or etiological fables. Nor is it mere reproduction or preservation of the present by a master-concept, an image which becomes the norm of behaviour. This social stereotype, watered-down by propaganda and publicity, is illusion and alienation. Its tendency is not to advance history but to halt it by simply giving a recognisable form to desire, and leaving man to re-volve within the closed circle of instinct. This stereotype takes a great number of different forms, from Hitler's racial propaganda or eroticism as a means of advertising, to the debased substitute for the mythical hero we find in the 'idol' which offers youth the compensating illusion of an alienated life, of a vicarious life, through the inflation of the myth: Soraya for Bérénice, Brigitte Bardot for Aphrodite.

There are myths which do us no service, or which do us a

disservice. They lead nowhere. There are others which direct us to the creative centre of ourselves, which open up continually new horizons and help us to go beyond our own confines. There are closed myths, and open myths, which latter are the only truly authentic myths.

We shall confine the name of myth to every symbolic story which calls man back to his true nature as creator, as being, that is, defined in the first place by the future he constructs and not by the past of the species, which urges him on simply by instinct and desire.

Such myths are not necessarily the products of a primitive mentality. There are contemporary myths which are the product of reason.

From its very beginning, myth is the language of transcendence, and that in its humblest form: man's transcendence in relation to nature.

It entails a double severance from the given: from external nature and from our own nature. Here Wallon's analysis (see above, pp. 55-6) coincides with that of Van der Leeuw: it is 'a return to the fundamental: the man who "stands on his own feet" and can say "no" about what is given to him as reality' (*L'homme primitif et la religion*, p. 199).

Marx asks us to explain in this way the enduring fascination through the centuries of the great myths of Greece, as expressing the healthy infancy of man, refusing to define reality solely by the *anankē* of the order existing in nature or society, whether it be Prometheus, Icarus, Antigone or Pygmalion.

In every great myth, whether poetic or religious, man regains his own transcendence in relation to every given order.

This, moreover, is based on the specifically human dimension of labour: the presence of the future as the leaven of the present.

If, from this point of view, we wish to conceive the relation of myth to time, we cannot do so as Mircea Eliade does, who, in his essays on magico-religious symbolism, speaks of what he calls 'escape-from-time techniques' in the Indian myths.

The characteristic of the great myths as an 'opening into transcendence' is more *mastery* of time than *escape* from time. The 'golden age' of myth allows man to relive the dawn of the world, the moment of creation; it allows him to comprehend himself not simply as a fragment of the cosmos, caught up in the web of its laws, but as capable of transcending the cosmos and intervening in it as creator.

Prometheus or Antigone (just, moreover, as the prophets of Israel or the gospel narratives) tell us that a new start is possible; I can begin my life over again and change the world. In this lies what is most valuable, as Paul Ricoeur says, in the 'power of interrogation' which the myth possesses. Here we cannot contrast myth and kerygma. Myth is necessarily the language of kerygma. When Bultmann, in his *Primitive Christianity (Das Ur-Christentum im Rahmen der antiken Religionen)*, endeavours to read the essential message of Christ, he shows that, unlike the Greek conception of the 'cosmos' of which man is a fragment and a moment, Christ comes to reveal to each man that the present is not the necessary link between the past and the future in the woven fabric of a destiny: 'The present is the time of decision.' Transcendence is the possibility of an absolute beginning. Speaking at the Strasbourg meeting from the Catholic point of view, Fr. Karl Rahner came very close to Bultmann's position on this point, when he defined Christianity as 'the religion of the absolute future.'

If I try to interpret what Bultmann or Rahner says, speaking as a Marxist—as someone, that is, who believes that transcendence is not an attribute of God but a dimension of man—then I find in every myth the reminder of this transcendence, and the summons, addressed to man, to exert his power of historical initiative.

The meaning of history was born with the first man, the first labour, the first project. This meaning is enriched by all human projects. There always remains a task and a creation to be accomplished. It is this that distinguishes the Marxist conception of history from that of Hegel; for the latter the meaning of final history is already present from the very start, and so the whole of human history is changed into a false history, being no more than the more or less conscious quest for this fulfilment.

Myth, therefore, is not a technique of escape from history, but rather a reminder of what is specifically historic in history: the act of human initiative. Aristotle suggested this in his *Poetics* (1450b, 1453a) in connection with tragedy: tragedy is not the imitation of just any action, but of an action which is at the same time a paradigm or ordered and completed whole, and has its own time-quality. (This, perhaps, is the precise opposite of what has come to be called 'the new novel' —but that is another matter.)

The mythical hero is the hero who is conscious of a question put to man by an historical situation, and sees in it its human significance (that is, transcending the situation), and whose victory or even failure makes us realise that we are responsible for solving the problems of our own time: this is the case with Hector or Ulysses, as it is with Pantagruel, Don Quixote, Faust, or Jean-Christophe.

We cannot, then, say, as Freud does in *Totem and Taboo*, that mythology is to the group as the dream is to the individual. The dream is only the expression of a pre-existing reality, the myth is a summons to overstep our confines. It is what Baudelaire said of the work of Delacroix: 'An education in greatness' (Bibliothèque de la Pléïade, Paris, 1961, p. 1117).

Paul Ricoeur has tried to restore a new, forward-looking, dimension to Freud's conception, a tension towards the future; this he does in his dialectical theory of interpretation whose opposite poles, he says, are 'archaeology and teleology' (p. 476): of these interpretations, one is directed towards the re-disclosure of archaic significations, and the other towards the emergence of representations which anticipate our spiritual adventure (p. 498). However, for all the generosity of mind shown in the attempt to look beyond Freud's retrogressive analyses and find in him, at least in a latent form, the progressive and forward-looking movement of Hegel's *Phenomenology of Mind*, we still come up against the real limits of Freud's naturalism. Paul Ricoeur himself puts this in the most pregnantly significant terms when, in appraising the pros and cons of his double interpretation, he writes, 'It is with images originating in unsatisfied desire that we give form to our ideals' (p. 479).

So long as we look for the matrix of myth in desire and not in labour, we shall never be able to progress beyond this point of view.

To my mind, it is a misunderstanding of the mythic symbol in relation to the oneiric.

While Ricoeur maintains the thesis of the functional unity of dream and creation (p. 499), he emphasises, it is true, that the work of art is not the mere projection of the artist's conflicts. He brings out at least two differences: the work of art is a dream that conveys social values, and it calls for the mediation of the craftsman's work.

The difference goes further: there is no functional unity between dream and creation.

In creation, labour does not come in as a second moment, exclusively in the form of the craftsman's work. It plays the leading and constituent part in the genesis of the myth, which is one moment of it. Animal work is based purely upon the continuance of desire and the needs of the species, but what characterises specifically human labour is the emergence of the project, the creation of a *model*, which becomes the law of action.

What constitutes the specific nature of the mythic symbol in relation to the oneiric, is just this emergence of the model.

Lévi-Strauss writes that 'the object of the myth is to provide a logical model for the solution of a contradiction,' and he adds, 'one day we shall perhaps discover that the same logic is at work in both mythic and scientific thought.' When he says this, I am disturbed by only one word in his definition, the word 'logic'; for this suggests that the model can be reduced to the concept, whereas the 'muthos' cannot be reduced to the 'logos'.

With this reservation, however, we must be grateful to Lévi-Strauss for emphasising the functional unity of the myth and the scientific hypothesis, in the notion of the 'model' which includes them both. At the conclusion of his fine book on the Greek gods (*Les dieux de la Grèce*) André Bonard sets in their correct perspective the creations of Homer, Hesiod, or Aeschylus. 'The poet,' he says, 'does not invent; he has no right to invent the stories of the gods entirely out of his own head. At the same time we cannot say that he invents nothing. *He invents in the same way as a scientist formulates a hypothesis.* He imagines in order to account with accuracy for reality as he apprehends it' (p. 159).

Hector or Oedipus Rex, like the stories of the gods, are questionings about the meaning man can discover in his life or give to it. They are not only an *expression* of what he *is*; they also ask him what he can achieve and summon him to go further.

Psychoanalysis has exhausted its virtue when it leads us to consciousness of self, whereas the myth is creative of self.

That is why myth can no more be reduced to Hegel's phenomenology than it can be to Freud's psychoanalysis.

Even if a certain functional unity can be found in the mythic model and the scientific hypothesis, the former is a model whose specific character is defined by its *language*. In my view, it is the failure to recognise this specific character of myth which limits Hegel's aesthetic, as it does his philosophy of religion.

The exclusive privilege accorded to the concept which, in absolute knowledge, will make man and his history perfectly transparent and complete, leads to reducing religion and art to no more than inferior modes of knowledge, expressing in images what philosophy will exhaustively express in concepts.

Provided we distinguish myth from allegory, which has an illustrative but not a creative or interrogative role, what myth tells us in symbols cannot be reduced to a story expressed in concepts. This difference is fundamental.

Pavlov distinguished a first system of signalling constituted by sensorial stimuli, the signal in this case being simply the part for the whole, like the smoke for the fire. What he called the second system of signalling was language, constituted by words, and reaching its full development in the concept. We might call the symbol, after the sensorial signal and the word, 'the third system of signalling'.

This, too, expresses a form of man's relation to the world. It entails an enrichment of the conception of the real: reality is more than a nature that is given to us, with its own necessity or *anankē*; it is this second nature created by man, by technology and art, and also all that does not yet exist; it is the constantly shifting horizon of the human potential.

For a Marxist, the myth cannot be conceived solely as a *relation to being*; it is also a *summons to making*. The symbol does not send us back to an all-embracing being in which we live and move and have our being. It is the language in which a need is expressed. It reveals to us not a presence but an absence, a lack, a void which it calls upon us to fill.

This third system of signalling is essential 'poetic' in the strongest sense of the word: the continued creation of man by man.

It is in this sense that a Marxist interprets the great myths both of art and religion as the language of existence.

These myths testify to the active, creative, presence of man in a world that is continually being born and growing. Every great work of art is one of these myths. From Cervantes to Cézanne, or from Paul Klee to Brecht, what is called in them 'distortion' of the real is in fact mythical image of the real.

When a still-life by Cézanne or one of Paul Klee's works gives us the feeling of an equilibrium that is on the point of collapsing and is only maintained on the edge of catastrophe by man's major act—artistic composition—we have there the plastic expression of the inexhaustible truth that the real is not something given to us ready-made but is a task that has to be accomplished. It is a reminder or an awakening of responsibility, a reminder of what man is. This is the meaning of Stendhal's saying, 'Painting is simply a construction of ethics' (*Histoire de la peinture italienne*, p. 338).

Thus, at the level of this third system of signalling, that of the symbol, of the language of need and absence, transcendence and creation, man effects a conversion that is even more profound than the earlier; the transition from the first to the second system, that is from the lived to the concept, called for a 'de-centration' of man, the abandonment of the sensible and lived point of view in order to attain, with the concept, a progressively more de-centred vision of the universe. The pictures of the world presented in turn by Ptolemy, Copernicus, and Einstein, provide us with striking illustration of the 'de-centration' which is thus effected by scientific thought.

The transition, however, from the concept to the symbol is even more demanding: it is a challenge to every order that is finite in the sense of finished, and the consciousness that it is finite only by comparison with the infinite. In this case we meet *conversion* in the strict sense of the word: until then we were orientated, through our senses or our concepts, towards what is already made, but now the myth calls on us to turn towards what still has to be made. It tells us that we must not be merely makers of things or calculators of relationships, but must be givers of meaning and creators of the future. The symbol demands this detachment from being, this transcending of being in meaning and creation.

The third signal-system forbids us to be unthinkingly attached to what already exists. To define myth as the language of transcendence is in no way a negation of reason; it means going beyond it dialectically in a reason which is conscious of always transcending itself in the provisional orders it has already established.

It will, perhaps, seem surprising that such cardinal importance should be attributed in this book to the role of myth in aesthetic creation and religious experience.

If, when reading the word 'myth', one follows the usual tendency, that is sufficient to cause one to confuse the mythical with the unreal, and myth with mythology, and both with arbitrary and puerile fable-mongering.

At this point I can already hear the Catholic integrist—in the exact sense defined earlier—exclaim at this attack on his faith. Nevertheless living theology from Père Laberthonnière to Karl Barth, has sanctioned the making of the necessary distinctions, and, following Bultmann, has allowed us to show that the required 'demythologising' of faith could not lead either to its relegation to mythology (confusing it with the religious—cultural or institutional—forms in which it may have been clothed), or to the exclusion of myth, but rather to the apprehension of its true nature. Mythology is the dogmatic corruption of myth, just as scientism is the dogmatic corruption of science. Mythology is the claim to retain only the letter of the myth, and not its spirit, the matter of the symbol and not its meaning. Antigone would make little impact upon us if she were no more than her obstinate determination to carry out Polynices' funeral rites, and the Resurrection of Christ would not have been revolutionising men's lives for the last two thousand years if it involved no more than a problem of the physiology of cells or of re-animation.

The myth, freed from mythology, begins where the concept leaves off, that is, with knowledge not of given *being* but of the *creative* act. It is not the reflection of a being but the setting up of an act as an objective: and it is expressed not in concepts but in symbols.

It is the creative act apprehended from within, by the intention which inspires it. This knowledge, or this level of knowledge, has for its object, not the universal, but the personal and the lived. It gives meaning to creation and sets the creative act in motion. It is summons, it is act, and it is person. Neither Antigone, nor Hamlet, nor Faust can be confined within concepts; they can only express themselves in a manner of personal behaviour through a reactivation of the historical initiative of the hero.

Myth, then, in its highest sense, lies at the level of poetic knowledge and of man's free and responsible decision. It is only at that level, the level at which the creative act is grasped and choice is made, that the *meaning* of life and history can first be determined and disclosed. For we cannot be satisfied by discovering this meaning in the same way as we see a landscape from the top of a mountain: it is one and the same thing to *receive* this meaning through knowledge and to *give* it through action; to live it in myth, as awareness and responsibility; through understanding of past history, to survey the whole panorama of earlier development, and to share in the practical, militant, realisation of this meaning. In myth, order is manifest, in the twofold sense of harmony and command.

Conceived in this way, myth is not the opposite of concept, but its birth.

Since, through the construction of myth, art is an exemplary form of the creative act of man building his future, the working out of an aesthetic is not supererogatory for a Marxist.

Nevertheless, it is a difficult task, for the founders of Marxism, Marx and Engels, never systematically worked out the principles of an aesthetics. All one can find in their writings is limited judgments on this or that particular work of art, and a number of incidental comments on method. These are indeed valuable material, but in order to construct a Marxist aesthetics we must do more than just string them together. To adopt the purely scholastic way of accumulating quotations which are connected by deductions made in accordance with the laws of formal logic, would not enable us to find our way at the present stage of development of the arts.

We must therefore, follow a different procedure, if we are to allow Marxism to develop creatively in the domain of the arts.

A brief indication of Marx's tells us no more than that in order to initiate a systematic study of this problem it was his intention to start from Hegel's aesthetic, applying to it the same critical method as he applied to Hegelian philosophy in general.

The starting point of our thinking can only be the principles of Marxist philosophy, and what we have to do is to find out where an enquiry into aesthetics can be fitted into them.

We are concerned here not with a subordinate question, but with a consideration of the very spirit of Marxism; and our conclusions are of capital importance for its fundamental interpretation.

The problem of art is above all the problem of creation, and that is why any mechanistic or idealist distortion, and any dogmatic conception of the creative act, will have consequences in aesthetics that will be immediately perceptible.

Thus the conception of aesthetics is the touchstone of the interpretation of Marxism.

*

Two analogies can guide us in our search for the starting point of a Marxist aesthetics: the method worked out by Marx in *Capital*, which is his 'classical logic' applied to the particular case of political economy, and the method which he developed under the name of 'historical materialism', of the application of which he gave some brilliant examples, notably in *The Eighteenth Brumaire of Louis Bonaparte*.

At the outset of a study of an historical phenomenon, Marx

emphasises that it is men who make their own history, but that they do not do this arbitrarily.

Marx's starting point, accordingly, coincides with that of German philosophy, and above all with that of Kant, Fichte and Hegel.

This classical German idealism had the merit of bringing out the 'active aspect' of knowledge and, more generally, the role of man's creative act with such emphasis as to see the whole of history as a continued creation of man by himself. In contrast with this, Marx conceives this creative act in a new and materialist way. He stresses the constant reciprocal action between men and the beings existing in nature external to and independent of him, and he tries to discover how freedom emerges from nature at the level of human labour.

Thus while Marx parts company radically with idealism by ceasing to conceive labour solely in its abstract form as creation of concepts, he is also radically distinguished from mechanistic materialism which, failing to recognise the active aspect of knowledge and man's creative role, reduced knowledge to being no more than a passive reflection of being, and man to no more than a resultant or product of the conditions in which he has been formed and develops.

We find in aesthetics a transposition of these different forms of the theory of knowledge. Objective idealism led to a transcendent conception of beauty: for Plato, beauty was a characteristic of ideas or essences, transcendent in relation to man.

Subjective-idealism in some of the romantics, Novalis for example, made beauty a product or projection of the subject alone, and even a 'magic' creation of the individual.

Mechanistic materialism, in Diderot and, more generally, in the eighteenth-century French materialists, made beauty a property of things, and led to a naturalism which reduced the work of art to being an imitative *reflection* of reality, its sole concern being to choose and reflect what in nature has an elevating value as an example.

176

There is a radical distinction between Marxist aesthetics and these three conceptions, which derive from idealism, subjective or objective, or mechanistic materialism.

Rather, however, than define it by contrast, in an attack on these attitudes, it is better to start from what is central in the Marxist conception of man and the world, from the methodology of historical initiative and the creation it implies.

If art was born of labour, how has it come to have an independent existence?

Art is one aspect of man's activity as transformer of nature, that is, as worker.

Marx showed how man, in the process of labour, produced things to satisfy his needs. The sum of these things, which have no existence and meaning except for and through man, constitutes a 'second nature', a world of technology and of culture in the widest sense of the word: that world, for all that, is still a nature but a human nature, one that has been remade in accordance with human planes.

New relations are thus created between man and this nature which has been constituted from human products and institutions.

In transforming nature, man transforms himself. The creation of new *objects* corresponds to the creation of a new *subject*. Here we are a long way removed from the idealist conception, Fichtean, for example, of the relations between subject and object, which saw the subject alone as creator; we are equally removed, too, from the concept of dogmatic materialism— d'Holbach's—which believed that the object is something 'given', ready-made and immutable, of which the subject is no more than the passive reflection.

In fact, as man multiplies the means of satisfying his needs, so he creates new needs; and these, as Marx emphasised in the *Economic and Philosophical Manuscripts of 1844*, constitute the true human richness of man. The more man creates for himself needs which are specifically human, the more he raises himself above his original animality. These needs do more than express the immediate and unilateral relation with nature which characterises the animal level—the satisfaction of hunger or the repelling of aggression. They multiply man's relations with the world, and make possible an immediate form of knowledge, the form we have in science; and this can develop only to the extent that man is no longer hemmed in by immediate demands: he must be able to give himself some elbow-room in coping with his need. This makes possible the detour which uses the route of imagination, it allows the conscious operation of projects and devices for realising them, and finally the way round through the concept.

The conquest of the artistic, as of the scientific, dimension of human labour, calls in just the same way for a standing apart which interrupts the direct circuit between the need and the immediate object of its satisfaction. It is only then that a contemplation becomes possible, in which man sees in the object not only its content of utilitarian significance—for his nourishment or clothing, for his labour or self-defence— but also the expression it contains of man's creative act. The aesthetic attitude begins when man, to his delight, finds in the object he has created something more than a way of satisfying a need, when he sees it as a witness to his creative act. In the *Manuscripts of 1844* Marx speaks of the completely new character of the man who no longer works in accordance with the law of all species but works universally in accordance with the law of one species, the laws of beauty.

Art, the child of labour, is not necessarily something separate from it, and still less something opposed to it. On the contrary, it expresses the full significance of the object produced by labour; it expresses what I may call the 'double reading' of that meaning, since the object offers man a double 'usefulness': its immediate, economic, usefulness in as much as it is a product which is capable of satisfying a definite need, and its more generally 'human' (I would almost say spiritual) need, in as much as it is an object which reflects to man his own image as creator, an objectiorising of man's creative power, which arouses in him a feeling of joy and pride but at the same time, by constantly reminding him of this creative power, a feeling of anguished doubt and responsibility.

When bronze-age man drew a criss-cross pattern on his earthen drinking vessel, the decorative design acquired a certain autonomy in relation to the strictly utilitarian function of the object. Thereby man took delight in his own creative act.

A new need, hitherto unknown in the natural kingdom, had just been born; and, like all the other needs man has created for himself and all the means he has invented to satisfy them, it was to entail an enrichment and a profound transformation of the subject himself: his very senses were to develop and become more acute. The eye acquired the faculty of not only recognising a sign indicating the presence of a danger to be avoided or a quarry to be pursued, but of contemplating the object: of apprehending it, that is, not in terms of the satisfaction of a biological need, unilaterally, but of delighting in it in its totality, as an objectivising of man's subjectivity, of his fears and doubts, his hopes, and of his dignity as creator. The eye, in fact, then became a human eye. Similarly, when our ears distinguish the noise of a helicopter's engine from that of a jet, our sense of hearing has already been impregnated by a whole culture; still more so when, in a piece of orchestral music, it detects and is jarred by a wrong note from one of the violins. Our senses, as Marx put it, have become theoreticians: they sum up, in an apparently immediate reaction, the whole body of knowledge and power acquired by mankind as a species in the course of its history. Instead of the perpetuation of only the immediate and non-cumulative reactions of animal instinct, the whole culture of a society lives and develops in our senses.

This humanising of the senses goes with a corresponding humanising of the object. Through their relationship with this humanised nature, which is the work of human labour, the senses become human senses.

The structure and functioning of the sense-organs have a natural biological foundation, but they have become human as a result of a long historical and social transformation of mankind.

The development of the five senses, Marx writes, is the work of the universal history of human societies.

The subject who is equipped with these senses is not an isolated individual, but a social being who enters into a complicated relationship with nature through society; and this nature itself is a product of social labour.

*

Art, like labour, is an objectivising of man. Its products, like the product of labour, are human ends that have been attained; they are projects that have been realised.

Between art and labour, therefore, there is not that irreducible opposition that would permanently make labour be governed by vital needs that are necessarily servile, while artistic creation would be pure freedom. Kant's 'final purpose itself without final end', on which all idealist and formal conceptions of beauty are based, impoverishes both the notion of labour by reducing it to the realisation of strictly utilitarian and immediate ends, and that of art, which becomes a gratuitous activity and a form of play.

In labour and art we have the two extreme limits of one and the same creative activity which realises human ends and satisfies human needs: sometimes they satisfy particular needs, biological in origin but growing continually more complex and more socialised; and finally, they satisfy the need that is both the most general and the most deep-rooted experienced by man, the need to realise his own humanity through his creative act: the specifically human 'spiritual' need.

On the other hand, what is equally true is that in every

commodity society (which introduces alienation of labour through the fetishism of commodities), and still more in every society that is divided into antagonistic classes, in which relations of exploitation and domination aggravate and generalise alienation, a split or a cleavage is effected in the initially single act of labour.

With the birth of private ownership of the means of production, man, that is the creator, the worker, becomes a slave, a serf, or a proletarian, and no longer owns those means of production. It is then that the organic link is broken between the conscious end man assigns himself in his labour, and the means he puts into operation to achieve it. Thus the creator is cut off from the product of his labour, for it no longer belongs to him but to the owner of the means of production, the slave-owner, the feudal lord or the capitalist employer. His labour, therefore, is no longer the realisation of his own ends and personal projects, but that of another man's. So, in his labour, man ceases to be a man, that is, the person who decides the ends, and becomes a means; he is simply one moment in the objective process of production, *a means* of producing commodities and surplus value. Here alienation is *dispossession*.

In every régime based on private ownership of the means of production, the worker is cut off not only from the *product* of his labour, but also from its very *act*.

The master imposes on him not only the ends of his labour, but its means and methods. Physical movements and their pace are governed from outside the worker by the place he is assigned in the production line. They are designed in advance, stereotyped, in a completely dehumanised form, and at a rhythm that often becomes stupefying, by the tool or machine, until, in Marx's phrase, the worker is made into 'a flesh and blood appendage in a machine of steel'. Here alienation is *depersonalisation*.

The whole of the means of production existing at a given period in history, and the whole of the scientific and technical means of culture and power which they represent, are the fruit of the labour and thought of all preceding generations. When a man works, his activity embraces the whole of earlier mankind; his labour is the expression of man's 'species-life', of all the creations accumulated by the human species. When the means of production are in private ownership, all this patrimony, which contains the creative work of the whole of past mankind, of mankind as, in Marx's phrase, 'a species-being', is in the hands of a number of individuals who have at their disposal the inventions accumulated by thousands of years of human labour and genius.

Thus private ownership is the supreme form of alienation. 'Social power,' Marx was to say in *Capital*, 'has become private power in the hands of a few.' Capital is the alienated power of mankind getting itself up above men as a foreign and inhuman power. Here alienation is *dehumanisation*.

This alienation of labour leads inevitably to the separation in labour of what is a means for realising ends that the worker has not determined, from what is creation, the determination of ends; in every class society the latter is a class privilege. This divorce between alienated labour and creative labour is a source of mystification: alienated labour, which is in fact an historical phenomenon, appears as the 'natural', and in consequence the necessary and perennial form of labour, and creative labour, which is the definition of art, will be cut off from its earthly origins and appear as a gift from heaven, transcending human needs.

We may, then, draw up the main lines of a Marxist critique of Hegel's aesthetics as follows.

1. Marx adopts Hegel's key idea (borrowed, in fact, by Hegel, from Fichte) that man is the continued creation of man by man. However, unlike Fichte and Hegel, Marx does not conceive this creative act in the abstract and alienated form of spiritual creation, or the creation of concepts, or in the individualistic and romantic form of arbitrary creation in isolation.

From Marx's materialist point of view, man's creative act is concrete labour; it is a moment of the reciprocal action of nature and man, in which nature imposes his needs on man and man emerges from this nature through the conscious elaboration of his ends.

This concrete labour is at the same time social labour, which constitutes its values in history, with their historical continuity and their social objectivity.

Artistic creation is immanent in this labour; it is its supreme moment, in which new ends are discovered. It is not only a production of mind but a realisation of the complete man.

2. Unlike Hegel, Marx distinguishes *alienation* from *objectivation*. The latter is the act by which man, in producing an object, realises his own ends, whereas the former is the form assumed by objectivation in every economic and social formation in which the profit system prevails and, still more, in every régime in which labour power becomes a commodity. As Vasquez writes in his *Las ideas esteticas de Marx*, 'objectivation allowed man to rise from the natural to the human: alienation reverses this movement.' Such are the historical conditions that entailed the separation between the conception of the ends, which becomes the privilege of the ruling classes, and their realisation; all those who do not own the instruments of production become means for effecting the latter. From this fundamental separation, which is a product of class divisions, all other forms of separation are generated: of consciousness from manual operation, project from execution, manual labour from intellectual, labour from art.

3. Unlike Hegel, Marx does not regard art solely as a form of knowledge. For Hegel art (as, moreover, religion) is distinguished from philosophy only by its form and language. It expresses in images and symbols what philosophy expresses more perfectly in concepts.

It is just because Marx conceives labour not solely in its abstract form of producing concepts, but in its concrete form of producing new means which give rise to new needs, that he opens up for social man a boundless horizon of creation and transformation. Man can discover what is specific to art in its *object*, which is to satisfy not a particular need experienced by man, but his specifically human need to objectify himself as creator—in the precise sense in which Marx was later to say in *Capital* that in communism the free development of man's creative powers, released from physical needs, will become an end in itself. He can make the same discovery in the *language* of art, which is no longer the language of the concept, which always expresses a *reality*, that is, an object or a relationship which is already constituted, but that of 'poetry' (*poiesis*), in the deepest sense of the word: the language of myth, which expresses not a ready-made reality but one that is in process of being made, which is still incomplete, and in which a still unforeseeable future is present in embryo.

*

Thus Marxist thought in aesthetics makes it possible to demystify and de-alienate from their romantic or mystical variations, and so integrate, all that is most valuable in the studies of aesthetics that have been made in the last hundred and fifty years.

The modern concept of art was born of the affirmation of man's autonomy: art is not imitation but creation. A certain romanticism introduced a deviation into this idea by obliterating the boundary between the self and the non-self, between dream and reality; but that is only an aspect of romanticism.

To sum this up schematically we may say that the original source of the two currents of romanticism is to be found in Rousseau.

The first derives from the *Rêveries d'un promeneur solitaire*; this was to develop in the direction of a 'magical idealism', of which Novalis was the most typical representative, and its life was nourished by the dream of a mystical communion with nature.

The second derives from the *Social Contract*, starting from man's act in constructing his *culture* and his 'autonomy', in both the natural and the social world.

From this current comes our modern conception of art, through Rousseau, the French Revolution, and the classical German philosophy of Kant, Fichte and Hegel, of which Marx could say that it was the 'German theory of the French Revolution'.

Here again the starting point is Fichte.

Writing about the French Revolution in 1793, at the height of Robespierre's ascendancy, Fichte applied the method and the criteria of Kant's philosophy to the justification of the Revolution, as a vindication of the transition from theory to practice. Fichte identifies Kant's 'Copernican revolution' in the theory of knowledge, which created a new universe of truth from the free and autonomous act of thought, with the revolution effected in France, which instituted a new right, by which *historical initiative* was accorded to the citizen, and the freedom to obey only those laws he has made for himself or to which he has given his assent.

This identification, which is the basis of the primacy of practice or action, was to become the soul of Fichte's system.

What Fichte calls the 'pure ego' is what, in me, speaks and acts in the name of the whole of mankind. The creative act of the artist provides the model of this. 'The arts,' he says in his *Science of Ethics*, 'convert the transcendent point of view into the common point of view.'

Goethe develops this conception of art-creation in his 'Critique of Diderot's essays on painting': he writes, 'The confusion of nature and art is the malady of our age . . . The artist must establish his own kingdom in nature . . . and create from it a second nature.'

This conception of art, which lies at the origin of all modern aesthetics, spread to France at the beginning of the nineteenth century.

The transition, as Etienne Gilson has emphasised, was effected with Madame de Staël. She brought out, in the first place, the fundamental orientation of German idealism. 'No philosopher before Fichte,' she writes, 'had carried the system of idealism to such a degree of scientific rigour: Fichte makes the *activity* of the soul the whole universe . . . It was in virtue of this system that he was suspected of scepticism. He was heard to say that in his next lecture he was going to create God . . . the truth is that he was going to show how the idea of divinity was born and developed in the soul of man' (*De l'Allemagne*, part 3, ch. 7).

She then deduced the aesthetic consequences of this conception: 'The Germans do not, as is ordinarily done, regard the imitation of nature as the principal object of art . . . In this respect, their poetic theory is in complete agreement with their philosophy' (*Ibid*).

Thus was born the conception of *art-creation*. Borrowing it explicitly from Madame de Staël, Delacroix was to express it again more forcibly: 'In Madame de Staël I meet again what is precisely the development of my own idea of painting,' he writes in his *Journal* (26 January 1824). When he systematically developed his thought in his fundamental article on 'Realism and Idealism', he lifted from Madame de Staël, without even enclosing them in quotation marks, her key propositions on German philosophy and aesthetics, on realism and the moral role of art:

'Art is not imitation but creation.'

'Art should elevate, but not indoctrinate the soul.'

Later, Baudelaire, starting from Delacroix's work and his conversations with him, laid the foundations of all modern aesthetics, at the same time re-adopting Goethe's central proposition, the artist's creation of a 'second nature'.

It is commonplace in contemporary art-history to note the widening, in time and space, of the artistic horizon during the last hundred years, and the growing attention paid by artists, those who practise the plastic arts in particular, to non-western arts. This is true of the impressionists', particularly Van Gogh's, study of Japanese prints, of Gauguin's interest in the arts of Indonesia and the Pacific, Matisse's or Paul Klee's in Islamic and Persian art, and that of the sur-realists, the Cubists, Léger and, most of all, Picasso, in the arts of pre-Columbian America, black Africa, Asia and Oceania.

The interpretations, however, of this undeniable fact do not seem as yet to have brought out its underlying signifi-cance.

It is often explained simply as a need to escape or revolt, that is, as a merely negative reaction: the wish to shake off a tradition.

Sometimes it is added that when they reject the idea that only the art of classical Greece and the Renaissance can provide a criterion of beauty, artists who are exploring new roads are looking for a sanction or a confirmation for their new departure in other traditions; and these may be found either in time, by going back to romanesque or Byzantine or Sumerian art, or in space, by contact with non-western arts.

It is true enough that such considerations affect the in-vestigations of contemporary painters, but they are never-theless only a secondary aspect.

*

When the criterion of beauty no longer calls for reference to a reality external to the work, one that is defined once and for all and in accordance with the norms of Greek rationalism or the technical spirit of the Renaissance, it is the very notion of the real that is challenged. Its definition is seen more and more as a function of the historical development of man, of science, of technology, and of social relations: in short, as a function of man's activity.

Conversely, when once that has been accepted, the picture can no longer be regarded either as a mirror in which an immutable external world is reflected, or as a screen on which an eternal interior world is projected. It must be seen as a 'model' (in the sense the word bears in cybernetics).

187

It is a plastic 'model' of the relations between these two worlds, that is, between man and the world: a 'model' which varies at every period of history according to the powers won by man over nature, over society and over himself.

It is from this way of looking at the arts that the whole idiom of modern painting derives.

Drawing is less and less the outline of an image or the abstract sign of a feeling, and more and more the recorded track—the wake, you might say—of a movement or an act.

Colour is no longer necessarily the local tone of things, nor the impressionist play of sunlight and life, nor a symbol of purely emotional value: it takes on a constructive value, and creates a space that is no longer given but made.

Composition is no longer necessarily a variation of the scenic content, obeying the physical and geometric laws of things, nor a mere decorative or musical arrangement: it is the construction of a 'model' which expresses the structure of an act. It is no longer subordinated to external things or only to creative participation in the development of the world.

Thus the picture is an object whose value cannot be measured in relation to a world which it is taken to represent. It has value in itself, as a technical object has, but with this difference that its purpose is not to assist a particular action but, at every period, to provide a 'model' which expresses our power of creating or transforming the world, and our confidence in that power.

From that starting point there develops what one might call the working out of the 'plastic model' of universal humanism proper to our own time. The relations between man and the world, between nature and culture, are from now on no longer expressed by painters according to the exclusively rationalist and technical 'model' worked out in essentials at the Renaissance; they take their inspiration from relations conceived and expressed in another language by non-western artists. For all the diversity of their investigations during the last hundred years, what is common to them all and fundamental is the challenge to the essential postulates of the western conception of the world since the Renaissance.

The aesthetics that came to be accepted as traditional since that time was based on a conception of the world and of man, according to which man, as an individual, was the centre and measure of all things; he inhabited a world whose space had been defined once and for all by the geometry of Euclid and the physics of Newton. The laws of perspective, codified at the Renaissance, expressed this conception of the world and of man. Within this immutable framework the painter reconstructed sensible appearances and ordered them in accordance with laws which were regarded as both laws of nature and laws of reason.

Such was at least the theory; for the artists who in the last four centuries created the masterpieces of classical painting were great precisely by virtue of that element in their painting which escaped their principles. To take but one example, we have only to think of Leonardo da Vinci's *Trattato della Pittura*, which is an admirable witness to sixteenth-century humanism, but deals with the author's technique and not his art.

At the end of the nineteenth century and the beginning of the twentieth, painters rediscovered in non-western arts and by going back beyond the Renaissance, what had been lost for four centuries in western art. Instead of starting from sensible appearances and imposing order on them, they are fascinated by the opposite procedure, so common among artists of other civilisations, of starting from the lived experience of invisible forces and then creating plastic equivalents which can express them.

'To make visible the invisible,' as Paul Klee said, was to link up with the spirit of Byzantine and romanesque art, whose tradition had been, if not interrupted, at least obscured since the Renaissance.

Such a point of view brings out clearly the source of the

mistakes that are made whenever there has been an attempt to define realism, in a socialist régime for example, with nothing behind one but the criteria of realism that were produced by the Renaissance; an attempt at definition which at the end of the nineteenth century was already causing the most conservative bourgeois critics to see in what went before the Renaissance, with its conception of space, colour, and composition, nothing but the fumblings of primitives, and in what, after the Renaissance, challenged its postulates, nothing but the impotence and perversity of degenerates.

Our Marxist conception of realism must not follow the lead of what was most conservative and limited in bourgeois criticism, but embrace the heritage of all the great creative periods of mankind and carry them further boldly and creatively.

This is all the more important in that a dogmatic conception of historical and dialectical materialism has still further aggravated the consequences of the metaphysical conception of the worst bourgeois criticism: that which accepted as perennial and immutable the aesthetic postulates of the Renaissance.

To take simply three examples of mistakes in aesthetics which derive from a mechanistic distortion of historical materialism:

1. The application of the global concept of *decadence* in Marxist criticism. Marx himself scoffed at this 'pretentious folly' of the eighteenth-century French materialists, who on the strength of their mechanistic materialism argued as follows: we are superior to the ancient Greeks in our technology and economy, therefore our art is superior to theirs. Voltaire's *Henriade* is better than Homer's *Iliad*.

This argument sadly underestimates the relative autonomy of superstructures, and leads to the belief that a decadent social and economic régime can produce only decadent works.

This is not true even in philosophy: even the period that

has brought the collapse of imperialism has witnessed the birth of important works, from which we have much to learn: our Marxism itself would be the poorer if we still thought, for example, as though Husserl and Heidegger, Freud, Bachelard or Lévi-Strauss, had never existed.

Even more does this hold good in art: the period that brought the decadence of capitalism and the collapse of imperialism witnessed the flowering of impressionism, Cézanne and Van Gogh, the Cubists, the Fauves, and in literature a whole body of immensely valuable writing, from Kafka to Claudel.

2. This application of the concept of decadence is only one particular instance of a more general mistake: this consists in seeing in art no more than an ideological superstructure, and a mere reflection of an already constituted reality which is external to it. The mechanistic conception of reflection is as fatal for the arts as it is for the sciences.

No Marxist would have any doubt but that art is part of the superstructures and, as such, is tied up with class interests; but to reduce the work of art to its ideological 'ingredients' is not only to lose sight of its specific character, but also to disregard its relative autonomy, and to forget that the development of art does not keep in step with that of society.

Marx emphasised that there is no difficulty in explaining the historic links between the tragedies of Sophocles and the social régime in which they were produced; but we still need an explanation of how it is that even today, in a completely different régime, they can still give us aesthetic pleasure and are still recognised as models that cannot be surpassed.

3. A third mistake consists in explaining the enduring value of a work of art, irrespective of class régimes, simply by the fact that art is a form of knowledge. No doubt, as Marx showed, for example, in the case of Balzac, or Lenin in that of Tolstoy, great works have value as knowledge; but to reduce art to this aspect is once again to fail to recognise its specific

character. It is not enough to follow Hegel and repeat that art is a specific form of knowledge, for it is not true that art teaches us through image what philosophy and history teach us through concepts. I cannot 'translate' Don Quixote or Hamlet, or any poem or picture, or musical composition, into concepts: and this because the specific property of the work of art is precisely its being inexhaustible both in its *object* and in its *language*.

In its *object*, because it is man as an active being, as creator. When, as we said before, a still-life by Cézanne gives us the feeling of an equilibrium that is on the point of collapsing, and this world, reduced to a table, a plate and three apples, seems to be held on the verge of catastrophe only by man's major act—artistic composition—we have there the plastic expression of the truth that the real is not only a *given* situation, but a *task* to be accomplished. The work is an awakening to responsibility, a reminder of what man is: a creator, a responsible being. This is as true of the *Antigone* as it is of *Faust*.

The language of art is closely linked to its object. Like the latter, it is necessarily inexhaustible. It is creative of myths, that is to say of 'models' of man as he transcends himself, and, going beyond the concept, which expresses what is already made, it is poetry or symbol; in other words it is the unexpected encounter of terms which does not *give* us an already made reality, but points out to us, and offers us as a '*target*', a reality that is being made.

Thus art is knowledge, but knowledge specifically qualified by its object and its language. It is man's knowledge of his creative power expressed in the inexhaustible language of myth.

This concept of reality at which the work of art aims implies a realism that can undergo endless developments and renewals, just as can that of reality itself: a realism which is not simply a reflection of the reality but a participation in the creation of a new reality.

For a Marxist, the history of art is not *consciousness* of self, as Hegel thought, but the history of the *creation* of self.

If we recognise this specific character of artistic creation we shall reach conclusions similar to those we formulated for the sciences.

If reality has been defined dogmatically and definitively, we shall exclude from realism everything that is a new reality, and what we will have done will be to claim to have defined, or determined, criteria of reality or morality which are given validity once and for all.

On the other hand, the recognition of the creative role of art will mean that we not only accept but look for, in art as in the sciences, a fruitful *pluralism* of styles and schools.

It is from this great aesthetic movement that it becomes possible to begin the working out of a Marxist aesthetics: not in order to demand from the artist the illustration of short-term slogans, but to call on him to share in the building up of the future of man—and this he can do by starting from a clear consciousness of the laws of historical development in our own period, and from an acute awareness of his personal responsibility towards that development, together with a similar consciousness of what socialism is fundamentally. Going beyond the negative phase of the class war, in which socialism is defined by contrast with the past, it is the régime that can make every man a man, that is a creator, at every level: the economic, the political, and the cultural. To give the artist this consciousness is to help him to play his part in awakening men to consciousness of their human, and therefore creative, quality.

*

Although we have here an exaltation of the role of subjectivity, it by no means follows that we are abandoning the positions held by historical materialism. What we are doing is to denounce a pseudo-scientific claim, the dogmatic claim to entrench oneself in historical development, to possess facts which are conceived as incompatible and immutable blocks of matter, and to be also the architect who knows in advance the overall plan, like God the Father and his Providence in Bossuet's *Discours sur l'histoire universelle*, and finally to possess a legal code for the management of these materials.

This critique of history does not lead us into a wilderness of ruins: it does not mean abandoning the hope of a scientific history, but simply points out that history which claims to be scientific is not always so. Scientific history is not apologetics nor hagiography; nor is it a 'philosophy of history' still haunted by the ghost of Hegel's 'absolute spirit' under a new name. It is in the first place a human history.

It is a reflection of man and time. It does not start from a sceptical doubt, which is merely destructive and leads to despair, but by a methodical doubt, which as the etymology of 'method' indicates, leads somewhere: and what it leads to is a certainty more sure than that of credulity.

With man, time takes on a new rhythm and a new meaning. While nature's time is measured by the movement or transformations of matter, man's time (in as much as he is no longer only, like the other animal species, a being that adapts itself to nature, but a being that transforms it, and in so doing transforms himself)—man's time is measured by his decisions and creations.

These decisions and creations are not arbitrary; they are conditioned by his earlier decisions and creations. Man, however, is not simply a link necessary and in itself without value, between the past and the future. The present is the time of decision; it is the moment when man assumes his responsibility towards the outcome, with the consciousness that, while his act results from a past of which he is the inevitable fruit, at the same time he inaugurates a new beginning; that he creates new possibilities and new chances, and there is no web of causality so strong but that it is possible for him first to fray it and then to tear it apart. True scientific history is the history which takes into account the specific character of its object, which does not claim identity with the history of physics, of biology or astronomy, and which is a history of men as beings responsible for the future. A man's life is really 'historical' (and not biological) when it is made up of free decisions.

This conception of history is also a conception of life. Marxism, by inaugurating, in alliance with historical materialism, a new age of history, has provided man with new means for building his own future. Because its materialist conception of man and the world is based on man's creative practice, it is a methodology of historical initiative. At the same time, this conception of the world is a moment in the liberation of man.

When, under the claim of being scientific history, it becomes fixed in dogmatism—in a scheme of development divided into five stages, universal in value and immutable —not only is there a reversion to a 'philosophy of history', whose uselessness was demonstrated by Marx, but a new fate, and a new inevitability are given currency, with all the fanaticism in behaviour which is produced by dogmatism in thought.

The time of history is not this empty framework into which events and men must at all costs be thrust. If many of our actions are not our own or are no longer our own, as a result of a dialectic of 'alienation' and of the 'fetishism' the key to which was given to us by Marx, and the analysis of which we are still a long way from completing, then how can a personal existence have any real meaning? Is man simply a function of structure and conjectures?

This is a problem which the novelist has to face, since, as Elsa Triolet writes in *Le grand jamais*, he is 'his heroes' predestined fate'. To what extent can one predict a man's future as one predicts that of the hero of a novel?

Is not the novelist's time, made up of man's initiatives more than of what he has to accept, closer to human, *historical*, truth than the clock-time and calendar-time in which we try to enclose 'facts', forgetting just the essential point—that they are historic, and therefore human 'facts'? That they are 'facts' in the sense of things made or created, and not inert data.

The problem of man and time brings us back to that of art and realism.

Is the novel history, or is history a novel?

The answer is not a matter of personal caprice: a distinct choice has to be made in relation to time.

The novel is not a link in the chain of time. Like the myth, it is *in advance* of time, and, for the Marxist, that defines it as creation: specifically human labour is labour which is *preceded* by the consciousness of its end; it is preceded by the project, which becomes its law. The work of art is this global image of the world and of himself which man cannot achieve until he takes a decision and affirms himself as creator. A myth is a model of action which corresponds to a global vision of the world and its meaning.

Science reduces what is purely arbitrary in that construction; it can never destroy its roots, since the roots are man himself as creator: creator of projects, of decisions and acts, of myths, of his own history, creator of his art and of his future. This is the very definition of man; it is what distinguishes him from other animals and other things, of which he is a part.

The specifically human reality is this projection or project; it is what a theologian would call this transcendence. Through its forward-looking character, art expresses the essence of humanity. The work of art is human reality being made.

Any form of realism, then, is insufficient if it recognises as real only what the senses can perceive and reason can already explain. The true realism is not that which affirms man's *destiny* but that which concentrates more on his *choices*: for the strictly human reality is *in addition* all that we have not yet become; it is all that we project ourselves as being, through myth, choice, hope, decision and battle.

There is a time proper to things, which is measured spatially and includes man as one of its elements; and there is a time proper to man, the time proper to the invention of self, which is measured by responsible decisions. Thus the fabric of our life is woven from this double time; its drama and its beauty lie in this, that what is at stake is the victory of man's time.

Postscript

by way of introduction to a discussion of this essay, with a plea for indulgence towards its shortcomings

*

Seven years ago, in *Perspectives de l'homme*, a far-reaching survey of the great currents of contemporary thought, I introduced the debate into the book itself by asking the authors whose views were disputed, or their supporters, to reply to the interpretation given of their work. This procedure made possible an initial approach, and the steps taken in the same spirit by the French Centre of Marxist Studies and Research to inaugurate public discussions, together with its study-weeks (the *Semaines de la Pensée Marxiste*), were the starting point for a large-scale dialogue between living thinkers.[1]

This dialogue was initiated by French Marxists and, as a result of the particular conditions prevailing in France, it was above all in Catholic quarters that it developed. There was a sudden expansion when the encyclical *Pacem in terris* and later the Vatican Council showed the willingness of the most vital elements in the Church to enter into 'dialogue' with the world.

Carrying this into practice enabled the various participants to realise the profound meaning of this dialogue: it is neither

[1] Cf. *Marxisme et Existentialisme* (Paris, Plon, 1962), which reproduces the discussions at the first *Semaine de la Pensée Marxiste*; *Morale chrétienne et morale Marxiste* (Paris, La Palatine), which contains the shorthand record of the first important dialogue between Christians and Marxists at the Palais de la Mutualité in 1960; *L'homme chrétien et l'homme marxiste* (Paris, La Palatine, 1964), which sums up the main discussions that followed in Paris and Lyons.

a skilful, and at the same time polite, form of polemic en-
gaged in by dogmatic systems, all of which are equally con-
vinced that they alone possess the whole truth and whose
only tactical aim is to make the other party accept it; nor
is it an attempt to replace inevitable conflicts—in particular
the class war—by purely verbal confrontations, which are
regarded as an end in themselves; nor, again, the eclectic
and agnostic approach, which puts all the proposed theses
on the same footing, and holds that each of them contains
an equal portion of the truth. On the contrary, it is a method
of inquiry which allows our teaching to incorporate not only
every fragment of truth that may have emerged from different
theoretical positions, but also, and above all, to ensure the
living development of its own truth by taking into account
what, at every moment, is being born in its new presentation.
Thus dialogue between men aims, beyond itself, at dialogue
between men and the world they are building.

If *Perspectives de l'homme* constitutes a starting point, this
essay on twentieth-century Marxism makes no claim to be
a terminal point or conclusion. All it hopes to do is to draw
up a first provisional estimate of what Marxism can gain for
its own creative development from this dialogue. And this
will be in the first place the incorporation of the extremely
valuable heritage of researches and discoveries that, even
from a mystified or alienated position, other currents of
thought have been able to make—whether they be philosophical or religious doctrines, scientific theories or methods
of research, Christian thinking or reflection upon life, psychoanalysis or structuralism. In addition, Marxism will have the
further gain of becoming fully alive to the transformations of
knowledge, of the world, and of history which are developing in the twentieth century with unprecedented rapidity.

The very principle of this book is such that it cannot end
with a conclusion, since its aim is to understand the movement of thought and action and not to enclose them in a
concept or a complete system. Having reached, therefore,

the point where I should 'conclude' it, I realise how easy it will be to misunderstand it.

To reflect on what twentieth-century Marxism can be, is not to propose any 'revision' or 'supersession' of Marxism. Rather is it to recall, as against any attempt at revising or dogmatising Marxism, what was Marx's essential discovery a hundred years ago, and the part played today by that cardinal discovery in raising thought and action to the level of the new conditions in which they are exercised. It is to recall the requirements, as simple as they are essential, of living Marxism: in the first place, that Marxist materialism is dialectical, and secondly that scientific socialism is not a 'scientist' Utopia, but militant thinking and a guide for action.

To say that Marxist materialism is dialectical is to emphasise that, unlike all earlier forms of materialism, every man is other than and more than the resultant of the conditions which produced him. It was only thus that Marx was able to base a methodology of historical initiative on a materialist conception of the world. If the future were no more than the extrapolation of the past (even one conceived through a mechanistic conception of dialectical reversals and supersessions), if conceptual knowledge of existing *being* allowed an exhaustive deduction of the *act* to be performed in order to fulfil future history, then there would be no more history; there would only be a philosophy or even a theology of history, and all it would do would be to replace the divine Providence of Bossuet's *Discours sur l'histoire universelle* by the concept of a speculative dialectic of production relations.

Marx's signal virtue is precisely that he pin-pointed the coupling of historical science and historical initiative, without sacrificing either the rational to an abstract 'freedom', or human choice to the concept in which what already exists and what has already been accomplished are summed up and illuminated.

When Marx says that men make their own history, but

that they do so in determined conditions handed down by the past, which they have not created in their entirety, he is expressing the principle of a method which links dialectically the two poles of historical development. In this, he is not claiming to give us a definitive conclusion, a universal key which will unlock the secret of the past and infallibly open the gates of the future. It marks the starting point of an inquiry into the meaning, inexhaustible in both directions, of history. In the first place this extends into the conceptual analysis of objective conditions: for history is not only *made* by men, but *written* by them. Analytical exploration of the past and its synthetic reconstruction—if this history is scientific and not scientist and dogmatic—are like every scientific theory; they can be challenged, they can be overhauled in their entirety in the light of and as expressions of new discoveries. By this I do not mean simply the digging up of new sources of information and documents about the past, but also the opening up of new roads into history as it is being made (and not merely written) which shed new light on the ways in which transition is effected from one structure to another. For example, the national liberation of peoples who have for a long time been colonialised, the renascence of their own history (denied to them or made meaningless by colonialism), the unprecedented forms assumed among them by the transition to socialism, have made it possible to express with a new clarity the wider problem of the diversity and complexity of the forces of transition from one structure to another: what Marx has so admirably visualised under the name of 'the Asiatic mode of production', and Stalinist scientism had buried in its dogmatising on the 'five-stage' formula.

The recognition of this authentically dialectical and creative character in the progress of knowledge (including historical knowledge) through overall reorganisations, involves no questioning, in historical science any more than in any other science, of what has been definitively gained;

all such gains are preserved within new syntheses when the preceding thesis is dialectically superseded. On the other hand, it does rule out the aberrations of an over-simplified scientism, which claims to be entrenched in a system of completed concepts, and from them to deduce the whole of earlier and later history: just as before our time a mechanistic conception of determinism had led Laplace to maintain that he could deduce in physics all the earlier and all the later states of the world system.

In the field of action and men's historical initiative, of their *practice* in the strongest sense of the word, the abandonment of one of the terms indissolubly linked together by Marx in his materialist and dialectical conception of history would have consequences as disastrous as on the plane of theory. Action is not the conclusion of a syllogism or of a demonstration in elementary mathematics: when conceptual, scientific, analysis of objective conditions has been carried as far as possible, then responsible decision comes in. This is not an arbitrary choice: it is, on the contrary, based on scientific study, but it is not derived from it in the same way as technical application results, with nothing to carry forward beyond itself, from knowledge of existing laws.

To recall this is not to provide a solution to the problem; but it does express the problem and show that there will never be a complete and definitive answer.

We can never repeat too often that we must emphasise the necessity of keeping hold of both ends of the chain, of maintaining, that is, the dialectical character of Marxism.

All Marxism's vicissitudes, during these last twenty years, have been caused by abandoning one or other of the aspects of historical dialectics.

To confine ourselves to France, there were, immediately after the Liberation, the numerous variations of a so-called 'humanist socialism' developed over fifteen years, from Léon Blum to Père Bigo, and from Maximilien Rubel to Père Calvez. Marxism was thus reduced to one of the forms of pre-Marxist socialism, utopian and moralistic. Henri Lefebvre proposed a new 'reading' of Marx, based on a 'return to Hegel', and making Marxism a renascence of the 'Hegelian left' and its philosophical 'communism'.

Against these various idealist retrograde movements we have opposed, in philosophy, the bulwark of a sketchy materialism, which often was no more than a barely modernised restatement of eighteenth-century French materialism or of Jules Guesde's and Paul Lafargue's polemical simplifications —when it was not positivism or scientism. In this respect, the most characteristic works were the successive re-issues, in the form of a 'Manual', of notes taken before the war during Georges Politzer's lectures, whose writings, some years earlier, had been the most forcible expression of Marxist thought. Another book which is characteristic of this approach, published in 1953 at the other end of those two decades, is my own *Théorie matérialiste de la connaissance*. As early as 1956 I forbade its re-issue. There is in it, as there is in the 'Manual', some useful material, but its general orientation is nevertheless pre-Hegelian and even pre-critical, and this, like all the writings of that period, brings us back to a pre-Marxist form of materialism.

The latest in date of the distortions of Marxism, illustrate, by their very symmetry, the consequences of abandoning one or other of the two aspects of Marx's conception: Sartre neglecting the essential element in scientific socialism by over-emphasising subjectivity, and Althusser, on the contrary, eliminating subjectivity and retaining only the conceptual aspect.

I shall not deal again here with Sartre's attempt, the significance of which I tried to bring out in my chapter on ethics, and shall confine myself simply to recalling that it cannot be regarded as an attempt to 'complete Marxism on the subjective side'. There is no 'Sartrian variant of Marxism', as has often, with too little justification, been asserted. It cannot be denied that in our time Sartre's philosophy has forcibly raised the problem of subjectivity, and I have shown the necessity, for Marxism, of not underestimating its importance. But the answers Sartre gives cannot be included in the Marxist point of view; they are, in fact, its negation.

From *Being and Nothingness* to the *Critique de la Raison dialectique*, Sartre has, indeed, been trying to express the philosophical conclusions to be drawn from historical experience of the part played by the working class and its renewed assertion that Marxism is the unsurpassable truth of our time; but in spite of this his conception of freedom is still metaphysical; it is still transcendent in relation to history, and fundamentally individualist. Since he thus defines freedom not as an increasing power gradually won by history, but as the abstract privilege of saying 'No' and inaugurating absolute beginnings, the boundary line, in Sartre, is still imprecise between the necessary recognition that the meaning of history is still open and the illusion that at any moment there is no saying what it may not become. This fundamental irrationalism in philosophy takes the form, in political practice, of an inability to distinguish at every moment between the real forces from which a human future can be secured, and speculations which are the fruit of impatience and impulse. In spite of Sartre's verbal recognition of the determining role of the working class and its party, and his desire to assist the forces of progress in the Resistance, and in the struggle against colonialism and personal power, his initial error takes the form, in his political activity, of some disastrous confusions: the fundamental confusion in 1956, for example, between a revolution and a counter-revolution, or the attempt to set up under the name of 'Democratic Alliance' (*Rassemblement démocratique*) a 'third force' whose uselessness he later realised, although he continually repeated the mistake of believing that he could effect progress by collaborating not with the working class and its party but with its opponents. The source of these mistakes and the impotence which derives from them is the same in each case: individual subjectivities do not provide a starting point from which one can distinguish real, objective, historical forces operating in the confrontations of classes and nations.

Althusser's 'theoretical anti-humanism', the exactly corresponding converse of Sartre's subjectivism, rests on the illusion of being able to entrench oneself in the concept and so treat structures and social relationships without reference to human options. This eliminates the 'active element' of knowledge so forcibly emphasised by Marx as being the 'subjective' (but in no way individualist) element of historical initiative—the active element of consciousness which is inherent in the very principle of a revolutionary party. Althusser's point of view loses what is fundamental in Marxism: the deep-rooted unity of theory and practice, in the Marxist sense of the latter term. Where it is not reduced either to the 'theoretical practice' of linking together concepts in sequence, nor to the purely 'technical' practice of unfolding the consequences of a system of already formed concepts in order, for example, to construct a machine.

'Practice', as the word is used by Marx and Lenin, implies both the element of conceptual analysis of the objective conditions of action, and the specifically human element (no longer merely technical, but 'moral') of the dialectical supersession and the break which calls for anticipation of the ends —with all that anticipation contains of risk, of responsible choice, and real historical initiative.

For Marxism, neither the concept nor freedom is constituted and defined, once and for all, outside history: that is outside men's works, outside man considered in the development of his history.

The 'theoretical anti-humanism' of Althusser's school is the specifically French variant of neo-dogmatism:[1] specifically

---

[1] Dogmatism, in the philosophical meaning of the word (as defined in Chapter 2) and not in cultural and political meaning. The latter is denial of freedom of research and creation, and rejection of a plurality of hypo-

French, because it claims to reject all that Marx inherited from Hegel, Fichte and Kant, and to rest upon a Cartesian conception of the concept with a new infusion of structuralism.

This French variant of neo-dogmatism carries the dogmatising of Marxism to very great lengths. For the Marxist dialectic it substitutes a Cartesian or Spinozist theory of the concept (whose hopelessly outworn character, when looked at in the light of contemporary scientific development, was emphasised over twenty years ago by Bachelard in his studies on a 'non-Cartesian epistemology'). This return to Descartes or Spinoza obliges the neo-dogmatists to remove from Marx the whole legacy of classical German philosophy which Marx and Lenin regarded as their prime source.

In this retreat from a materialist and dialectical philosophy towards a dogmatic rationalism in which the subject of history is no longer man but the concept, history is made without men (who are reduced to being no more than the medium which carries production relations); and ethics and, more generally, practice, cease to have any meaning and are expelled into the outer darkness of ideology.

The element of the concept, that is, of science already constituted, is a cardinal element in historical dialectic; but if this element alone is stressed at the expense of all the others, if the 'active element' of knowledge (of which Marx writes in the *Theses on Feuerbach*) is thus left out of account, the element of conscious anticipation of the ends in labour (of which, again, he writes in *Capital*); in other words, if the element of project and historical initiative is eliminated from human practice, then the neo-dogmatism of this 'theoretical anti-humanism' thereby eliminates dialectic, history and practice; it gets rid of all that is fundamental in Marxism.

theses at any given moment. The two aspects are often allied, but this does not mean that dogmatists may not be ardent supporters of conditions that allow free investigation.

Cartesianism and Spinozism, eighteenth-century French materialism, and classical German philosophy have all had their own greatness, and they are still inexhaustible sources of reflection and indispensable models of method for contemporary thought; but Marxism, which has to incorporate this wonderful heritage, cannot go back either to Descartes or Spinoza, to d'Holbach or Fichte, to Hegel or Feuerbach. What constitutes the revolution in philosophy inaugurated by Marx is precisely this: that for the first time he forged an unbreakable link between theory and practice, philosophic thought and militant action, for the transformation of the world: that he thus made theory an element in history being made.

Althusser's concepts of 'metonymic causality' and 'structural determinism' destroy historical dialectic at two levels: the emphasis laid on structure leads to a neglect of creativity

      (a) at the powers of production level
      (b) at superstructure level

Action (political action, for example) is conceived with the *application* of science as the model.

Most fortunately, although this neo-dogmatism has strongly coloured various intellectual reviews, it has as yet caused no deviation in the policy of the French Communist Party.

In this essay, I have done my best to relate every thought and every action to its starting point, and to comprehend them in their operation, while they are in process of formation. It is a very difficult matter to direct one's thoughts upon what, by its very principle, cannot be reduced to the concept: the concept in its nascent state, while it is still hypothesis, still a movement of the mind, an aim that is still fumbling; and the same applies to historical initiative of action while it is still project and provisional anticipation.

At this level there is a very serious danger of confusion. It will be easy to accuse of irrationalism, pragmatism and 'humanist' ideology, of abandoning Marxism, an attempt to reflect upon the concept and action when they are still being born in the melting-pot.

The concept is the sum total of verified and systematised knowledge at a given moment in the development of the sciences. It makes possible an objective synthesis of the known. Engels, for example, unfolded its magnificent panorama in his *Dialectics of Nature*. The error, for which neither Marx nor Engels is to blame, but which was introduced by some of their dogmatic and naïve followers, lies in confusing this provisional balance-sheet of science at one moment of its development with a definitive metaphysical extrapolation which would make it possible to unfold a philosophy of nature and a philosophy of history whose inflexible path is already drawn once and for all, and in which men, their creative act and their historical initiative, have no part to play.

For a Marxist, the meaning of life and of history is not the creation of the individual man, as existentialism suggests. This meaning is not laid down at once and for all and without us in a history which unfolds in accordance with the immutable laws of a Providence or the no less immutable (and no less theological) laws of a 'Progress' which is conceived in the manner of a metaphysical materialism (very close, moreover, to a metaphysical idealism, of which it is simply the inverted form). Certain scientist interpretations of Engels' *Dialectics of Nature* or of Teilhard de Chardin's *Phenomenon of Man* lead to forms of dogmatism that are very close to one another. The meaning of history is man's work, or rather the work of men in the totality of their history.

We can say, contradicting all 'existentialisms', that this meaning already exists, before us and without us, because the historical initiatives of early generations are crystallised today into products and institutions which create rigid historical conditions for the operation of our present initiatives, and radically exclude a large number of historical 'possibles'.

Nevertheless this meaning is still an open question, for the future still has to be created even though its creation must start from conditions inherited from the past. It is not already written down, and if we do not fulfil our task as men, that is, as creators, the possibility of the dialectical transcendence not being effected is by no means ruled out; there may well be, simply through the force of inertia of the past, a corruption of history; the contradictions that are undermining the world of capital, instead of finding their historical solution, may lead to disruptions which, at the present stage of the development of the techniques and the powers of destruction that man has conquered, could end in the collapse of evolution and the abolition of life. The game is not over; no move can be made without us.

Our conceptual analysis of the conditions in which our historical initiative and our decision have to intervene can be exhaustive; but that does not exempt us from making a choice and taking a risk. It is in this sense that there is 'transcendence', which simply means that there is a discontinuity between the human creative *act* and the *being* already realised, together with the concept which expresses the latter. This 'transcendence'—which is simply this discontinuity between creative human *act* and *being*, is not the attribute of a God, but the specifically human dimension of action. If 'transcendence' in the alienated and religious sense may be taken as equivalent to 'supernatural', then the authentic, no more than human, experience which covers the word is the experience of dialectical supersession of the continued creation of man by man which involves the relative discontinuity referred to: that discontinuity being the impossibility of reducing act, decision, and choice, to the conditions which produced them and the analytical concepts of those conditions.

In short, neither meaning nor value nor responsible decision can be interpreted at simply the level of the concept.

To understand what a Christian's faith can be, one has

to adopt the position in which to think that the world has a meaning and to hold oneself responsible for its significance are indistinguishable. This commitment of our whole being, both in theory and practice, is what is traditionally known as faith. The word can lead to many ambiguities, precisely because this faith is essentially dialectical: it is at once knowledge and action, being and act; it is both assurance and uncertainty, commitment and awareness of risk, dependence on the past and a breakaway which creates the future; and it is under the constant threat of alienation.

We have only for a moment to leave the ridge on which affirmation and challenge, belief and doubt, come together in unstable equilibrium, to slide down one or other of the two slopes. And then we see only the aspect of rupture, of transcendence, and are lost in fideism, in credulous acceptance of the supernatural and irrational; or, on the other hand, we see only the aspect of affirmation, of immanence, and entrench ourselves in the fatal inertia of an absolute knowledge, either in its theological or its scientist form—both variants of one and the same dogmatism.

The first road, to take an example, leads to Catholic integrism, whose essential characteristic is the confusion of what is fundamental in the Christian message with the cultural and institutional forms in which it has been expressed at a particular moment of its historical development: in other words, it is the confusion of faith with religion, it is to entrench oneself in what one believes to be an immutable truth which becomes in reality a mythology so soon as it ceases to be the living source of man's endless renewal, so soon as it is no longer a perennial summons to transcend a form that has been acquired, and inaugurate a future that is always open. We then have all the varying forms of a Christianity which is seen through Plato and Aristotle and, paradoxically, identifies their conception of the world and knowledge with what Bultmann calls the Christian *Kerygma*, that is, the Christian message and its preaching. This hel-

lenising and theocratic Christianity is not only, from the
theoretical point of view, completely out of step with the
theory of knowledge suggested to us by the whole of the
modern development of technology, science and the arts;
but, in addition, it serves, in practice, as an opiate. It hampers
human progress by contrasting this world and the other
world, combat and love, and so providing an excuse for all
the forms of conservatism to which it gives its blessing and
the 'fragrance of spirituality' (cf. Marx, *Early Writings*, pp.
43-4).

The second road, to take another example, leads to a
pseudo-Marxist dogmatism, whose essential characteristic is
the confusion of what is fundamental in Marxism with the
cultural or institutional form in which it has been expressed
or realised at this or that moment of historical development,
in this or that country or in this or that condition. It is the
confusion of science with scientism, in other words the reduction of science to science as already constituted, and the entrenching of oneself in a system of complete concepts. There
we have the essence of all dogmatic perversion.

The central aim of this essay on twentieth-century Marxism
is to fight this perversion by showing that Marxism contains
within itself, in its very principle, infinite possibilities of development and renewal; and that at every moment in history
these make it possible to be fully conscious of new conditions
of thought and action.

In order to achieve this aim it was essential forcibly to
stress—too forcibly, maybe, since it necessitated breaking
with an ingrained habitual procedure—the aspect of dialectical transcendence, with all the break and discontinuity
in relation to the past that it implies. This experience of break
and discontinuity, which is one of the specific dimensions of
the human act, has been lived by Christianity in the alienated
form of transcendence and faith. The alienated form it has
assumed in history cannot prevent a Marxist from trying to
disclose the authentically human reality and the real content

it conceals and which Marxism has to incorporate. That is why we insist so forcibly on analysis of the religious phenomenon. To fail to understand its essence or to simplify its nature, would make Marxism itself unintelligible to us.

That explains the emphasis on the problems of aesthetics. Consideration of the nature and characteristics of creation in the arts is an indispensable element in Marxist research and in the development of a living Marxism, for it enables us, by starting from a specially favoured experience, to appreciate the conditions of the creative act in general, and to distinguish 'levels' of knowledge; it prevents us, too, from entrenching ourselves dogmatically in being and the concept which expresses it, and enables us to understand that act is not the mere extension of being.

At this point the dogmatist will complain that this means the abandonment of reason and rationalism; in fact it is simply a question of not confining oneself to reason as already constituted: what we have to do is to take up our position at the level of a rationalism that is constantly being created; we have to be at hand wherever something new is being born, which has not yet been crystallised in the form of concept.

There is a Buddhist proverb which answers this dogmatic temptation: 'Point at the moon and the fool looks at your finger.'

Acknowledgements

The editions of major works referred to in this volume are listed below. The translator and publishers would like to acknowledge their indebtedness for permission to use quotations from them:

The Peasant War in Germany by Friedrich Engels, International Publishers, New York, and Lawrence & Wishart, London, 1957; *The Phenomenology of Mind* by Friedrich Hegel, translated by Sir James Baillie, Allen & Unwin, London, 1966; *Capital* by Karl Marx, edited by Friedrich Engels, in 3 volumes, Lawrence & Wishart, London, 1954-9; *Early Writings* of Karl Marx, translated by T. B. Bottomore, C. A. Watts, London, 1963; *The German Ideology* by Karl Marx and Friedrich Engels, International Publishers, New York, and Lawrence & Wishart, London, 1968; *The Holy Family* by Karl Marx and Friedrich Engels, translated by R. Dixon, International Publishers, New York, and Lawrence & Wishart, London, 1957; *Selected Works* of Karl Marx and Friedrich Engels, International Publishers, New York, and Lawrence & Wishart, London, 1968; *Being and Nothingness* by Jean-Paul Sartre, translated by Hazel E. Barnes, Methuen, London, 1966; *Existentialism and Humanism* by Jean-Paul Sartre, translated by Philip Mairet, Methuen, London, 1968.

Index

act; man's creative, 173-4, 176, 178, 180, 181, 183, 208; philosophy of, 66, 84, 130; and project, 98

aesthetics, 42, 71, 176, 212; form in, 69; Marxist, 174-6, 193, 212; Marxist critique of Hegel's, 182-4; non-Aristotelian, 77, 159; and realism, 34, 190; in the Soviet Union, 28, 29; traditional, 189. *See* art, beauty

Africa, 21, 35, 36, 46

'agape', 137

agnosticism, 50, 59, 127

alienation, 31, 34, 88, 99-100, 139, 154, 181-2, 195; and Christian love, 134-5; distinction from objectivation, 148, 183; and faith, 210; Marx's concept, 77, 122-3; and moral systems, 101; private ownership supreme form, 182; religious, 116-18, 120; and social stereotype, 165; and transcendence, 134

Althusser, L., 203, 205, 207. *See* anti-humanism

analogy, reasoning by, 71

anti-communism, 16-17, 152

Antigone, 81, 166, 167, 173, 174

anti-humanism, 205-7

Apelles, 63

Apostel, L., 70

Aragon, Louis, 64, 104, 121-2, 136, 141-2

Aristotle, 57, 59, 60, 64, 66, 158, 159, 210

Armenia, 32

art, 56, 95-6, 125; Byzantine, 187, 189; and concept of decadence, 191-2; and creation, 164, 174, 175, 177, 178, 184, 185-6, 193; inexhaustibility, 192; and knowledge, 191-2; language of, 184, 192;

modern conception, 63-4, 184, 185-6; non-Western, 186-7, 188, 189; romanesque, 189; and satisfaction of human needs, 178-9, 180, 184; sociology of, 72-3. *See* aesthetics, beauty

Asia, 21, 35, 36, 46-7

atheism, 106-8, 141-3, 160-61, 162

atomic bomb, 22

atoms, 45, 48, 67-8

Augustine, St, 108-9, 112, 130, 134

autonomy, concept of, 132

'auto-regulation', 63, 70

Averroes, 36

aviation, 24

Bachelard, Gaston, 37, 42, 64, 77, 95, 191, 206

Balzac, H. de, 191

Bannour, Wanda, 87-8

Barth, Karl, 159, 173

Batista, Fulgencio, 16

Baudelaire, Charles, 168, 186

Bauer, Bruno, 116, 118

beauty, 62, 176, 178, 180, 187. *See* aesthetics, art

Beauvoir, Simone de, 88, 90-1, 92, 93

Becquerel, Henri, 40

being; and act, 173, 208; Greek concept, 159; philosophy of, 66, 84, 130

Bellarmine, Cardinal Robert, 138

Berkeley, George, 164

Bernard, Claude, 24

Bigo, Père, 202

biology, 24-5, 39, 46, 48, 60, 71

Blanquists, 11

Bloch, Joseph, 52

Blok, Alexander, 12

Blondel, Maurice, 159

Blum, Léon, 202

Boehme, Jakob, 61

215